A LESSON FOR US ALL

D0279792

Drawing on unpublished documents, *A Lesson for Us All* tells the story of the intrigue and pressures that marked the introduction of the national curriculum – the most sweeping reform in education since 1944. Duncan Graham, as chairman and chief executive of the NCC, was the man charged with introducing the new curriculum into the 24,000 state schools in England and Wales from 1988 to 1991 under three Education Secretaries – Kenneth Baker, John MacGregor and Kenneth Clarke.

In collaboration with David Tytler – former Education Editor of *The Times* – he tells of the struggles with ministers, civil servants and teachers to bring in the national curriculum on time. He examines in detail the arguments and compromises that surrounded the reports of the working groups in the various subjects before the introduction of statutory orders. Finally, he tells of the pressures which led to his own difficult decision that the time had come to leave, and he looks to the future asking whether the national curriculum has any chance of achieving its aims of raising standards by ensuring that all children are given a broad and challenging education.

Duncan Graham has worked as a teacher, a lecturer in higher education, and in administration. While County Education Officer in Suffolk he was closely involved nationally on curriculum development, the Burnham Committee and Teacher Appraisal. In 1987 he was the first education officer to become chief executive of a major county council when he moved to Humberside. The following year he was invited by Kenneth Baker to assume responsibility for the introduction of the national curriculum by becoming chairman and chief executive of the National Curriculum Council. He is now a consultant and visiting Professor at the School of Education, University of Manchester. **David Tytler** writes regularly both for *The Times* and the *Guardian*. He was the Education Editor of *The Times* from 1988 to 1992, and has held senior executive positions on several national newspapers including *The Times* and the *Daily Mail*. He lives with his wife and youngest daughter in South London, is Chairman of Governors at a local state primary school and a Governor of a grant-maintained selective school for girls.

A LESSON FOR US ALL

The making of the national curriculum

Duncan Graham with David Tytler

London and New York

First published 1993
by Routledge
11 New Fetter Lane, London EC4P 4EE

Simultaneously published in the USA and Canada
by Routledge
a division of Routledge, Chapman and Hall Inc.
29 West 35th Street, New York, NY 10001

Printed and bound in Great Britain by
Mackays of Chatham PLC, Chatham, Kent

Typeset in Palatino by LaserScript, Mitcham, Surrey

British Library Cataloguing in Publication Data
A catalogue reference for this book is available from the British Library.

ISBN 0–415–08928–X (pbk)

Library of Congress Cataloging in Publication Data
has been applied for.

For Kate and Kirsty

CONTENTS

PREFACE

The National Curriculum Council was set up in August 1988 by Kenneth Baker, the then Secretary of State for Education, to establish and review the national curriculum introduced in the Education Reform Act 1988 for all state schools in England. A parallel body was formed in Wales. Baker appointed Duncan Graham to the twin posts of chairman and chief executive of the NCC which he held until his resignation in July 1991. This book is Duncan Graham's view of those three years. The book strives to be objective, although doubtless there will be other views, other conclusions. From any perspective, there are lessons for us all.

DGG/DT
Appleby
Cumbria
August 1992

ABBREVIATIONS

BTEC	Business and Technician Education Council
CDT	Craft, Design and Technology
DES	Department of Education and Science
LEA	local education authority
LMS	local management of schools
MSC	Manpower Services Commission
NCC	National Curriculum Council
NCVQ	National Council for Vocational Qualifications
NVQ	national vocational qualifications
PC	profile component
SAT	standard assessment task
SC	Schools Council
SCDC	School Curriculum Development Committee
SEAC	School Examinations and Assessment Council
TGAT	Task Group on Assessment and Testing
TVEI	Technical and Vocational Education Initiative
WCC	Whole Curriculum Committee

1

BIRTH OF A REVOLUTION

The Secretary of State for Education, Kenneth Baker, produced a malt whisky before offering me what he described as one of the most important and influential jobs in British education. There were no such pleasantries from his successor three years later when frustration with the growing gulf between practical reality and political imperatives led me to decide that the time had come for me to leave the post of chairman and chief executive of the National Curriculum Council.

I fell into the two-headed job almost by accident after a lifetime in education. Despite having worked in what is sometimes disparagingly called the education establishment since the late 1950s, I have never felt a part of it. We all have our own definitions of the education establishment, from the critical and negative view of some Conservative politicians to an idealist picture of great thinkers planning a bright new future for our children.

My own definition is rather more prosaic, seeing the education establishment in the 1960s and 1970s as a number of teachers working in teacher centres all over the country linked with equally well-intentioned local authority advisers and teacher trainers and concerned together in a benign conspiracy, reinventing a thousand wheels a day.

They became hooked on some perfectly respectable philosophies, such as child-centred education and learning by doing, basing all teaching on arousing a child's interest which resulted in a rush to teaching by projects rather than the more formal subject-based lessons of the past. There is nothing inherently wrong in any of these methods: indeed, as a teacher trainer in Scotland in the 1960s I was part of the primary revolution that moved children out of serried rows in front of the teacher learning by rote and instruction into small groups learning by discovery.

All of these new methods, however, have to be used as part of a balanced curriculum and must not become an end in themselves as they did in some schools through the 1970s and 1980s. As chief education

1

officer in Suffolk during the 1980s, I could see that most teachers were caught between the new methods and the old ones in a feeling of uncertainty. The problem, however, did not rest with them but with a small number of their more extreme colleagues who were grabbing the headlines with their over-enthusiastic support of the new methods. As a result, the public perception was that children were spending no time on the three Rs but were all playing in sand trays. At the same time, Her Majesty's inspectors of schools were saying that people were still doing too much of the three Rs and that children were being given too narrow an education, which led to frustration and boredom which in turn resulted in a drop in standards across the board. The ultimate effect was that whatever the reality, many parents thought that nobody was doing any grammar, nobody was doing any tables, nobody was being extended, expectations were too low: the familiar litany that has spawned the battle slogans of the right wing.

While few teachers were really into the extremes of progressive theories, the majority were not convincing people that they were teaching a balanced curriculum covering the basics that are now being demanded. The public perception was of a system going rapidly downhill and that is the key in all the reforms that were to follow in the 1988 Education Reform Act.

In addition to the revolution in some of our classrooms, the education of many of our children at that time was clearly not geared to industry and commerce in providing the recruits they wanted. Industrialists said that education was irrelevant to modern needs in not teaching sufficient practical skills. The arguments led to the trench warfare which lasted from the 1960s through to the 1980s and was unique to Britain. Industrialists and educationists fired shells at each other, with the industrialists saying that nobody could read or write or add up while educationists took the view that education was so pure that it must not be sullied by entrepreneurial nastiness. The awful thing was that both believed they were right no matter how wrong they clearly were, like the household name industrialist who was convinced that 83 per cent of children left school illiterate.

There was no need to be alarmist about education but it was necessary to be concerned that some schools were failing their pupils while others were doing too little to correct the false impression of what was really happening in their classrooms. The dialogue between educationists, the public, industry, commerce, and the politicians went disastrously wrong. The politicians were beginning to believe that education should be more geared to the needs of the world of work, while the educationists clung to a more romantic view.

The two sides were not to come even close until a decade after the 1976 speech made by James Callaghan, the then prime minister, at Ruskin College, Oxford, in which he touched on a number of the issues. The educational establishment took little notice of what the prime minister said and continued to head off in its own direction, seemingly unaware of the growing pressure for change in two vital areas. The first was a new demand for efficiency and value for money; the second was for a relevant curriculum.

Some local authorities in the 1960s and 1970s were clearly uninhibited by resource problems until in 1975, Anthony Crosland, the Labour government's environment secretary, announced that the party was over. Now local government expenditure was to be limited, a policy that led to controls in education expenditure and ultimately to the current debate on whether or not we should, as a country, reinvest in education, and for what outcomes.

Much of this argument could have been avoided if, as they are now beginning to be, people had been more practical about money. State school heads, for example, are now as conscious of the need to balance their budgets as the heads of independent schools; university people now think much more clearly about the cost effectiveness of what they are doing. Certainly in the 1960s, my own experience as a fledgling administrator was that money was not a problem. There was no concept of cash-limiting: supplementary budgets were easy to achieve. Until relatively recently, most people in education felt that money had to come if they said it was required. There was no need to justify on a balance sheet the cost effectiveness of what was being done.

The second concern, and critical in the development of the national curriculum, were the extreme doubts some people have always harboured about the relevance of the curriculum. It has long been watered down, a sort of romantic Matthew Arnold curriculum largely unconcerned with what children would do when they left school. One result of all this was that whereas the Germans and others went for technology in the late nineteenth century, we did not. By the 1940s there were about 200 technical schools in England as against 2,000 in Germany.

By the time of Callaghan's Ruskin speech, in which he called for a core national curriculum, I and many others had become even more convinced that we were serving the less able children badly by watering down what we taught them while the education of able children was very narrow and academic. The argument about A-levels continues. The examination still primarily serves the needs of universities, being based on the level a candidate has to reach to start a three-year first degree at the age of 18. Only a relatively small proportion of the population is ever going to do that while the rest have to suffer the consequences. How different it would be if the system had been set up for the average pupil rather than the top few per cent.

Ruskin forced a number of people to the realisation that things were not well. There was the start of the standards argument and the debate about why other countries were doing better than Britain. There was an ill-defined feeling of malaise which led to a growing belief that education was primarily a means to an economic end. Western countries could see that their economies were sliding downhill in comparison with the emergent nations, first Japan and latterly Korea, and that education was an important component of that success. The contrast between their educational success in terms of crude standards and ours was linked to all the other economic indicators and we reached the point where politicians were beginning to talk about the need to reform what was being taught in our schools, particularly in vocational terms to make it relevant to all children and to industry.

Ruskin was a seminal speech, touching on some of these fears. Callaghan did put his finger on the nub of the difficulties – a mixture of the things that were wrong and of a failure in communications. These two strands are very important: the perceptions were one thing, the realities were another but added together they led to the growing political feeling in the 1980s that something had to be done. The warning shots were fired and a range of changes were introduced before the 1988 Education Reform Act which, had they been left to flower, might have solved the problems.

In 1981 the Department of Education and Science issued a circular (6/81) to local education authorities telling them they had to have a curriculum policy, the first time that all the authorities were actually told that they had a role in planning what was taught in their schools.

When I went to Suffolk in 1979 the thing which most shook me was the feeling that education committees and chief education officers had little to do with the curriculum. Some advisers there told me that, as chief education officer, while I could be an honorary member of the curriculum team it was not really my business. This was in marked contrast to my experience in Scotland.

Although it appears that the Education Department did not know what to do with the curriculum policies when they arrrived, and locked them away in a room, the circular had a very great effect on local authorities and schools. Together they had to develop curriculum policies which were required to be clear both about content and teaching style and, by implication, had to involve sharing the curriculum with parents and businessmen. This was one of the big steps towards putting things right because the disadvantages of the decentralised English system now outweighed the benefits. When I came south, the best schools were better than I had ever seen, being more imaginative and less subject-orientated than Scottish schools. Equally, when it came to the worst, I had never seen schools as depressingly poor. This was not because people were malicious but because of incoherent curriculums, a scattering of high profile eccentric teaching methods, and the totally soft-centred belief that children would learn if you left them to it, that children could somehow learn to read by osmosis. The biggest single problem facing education in England was that there was no nationally agreed curriculum with recognised standards. The change ordered in 1981 began to put that right. In addition, secondary schools were greatly helped by the introduction in 1983 of TVEI, the Technical and Vocational Education Initiative, which emanated from a very odd stable, the Manpower Services Commission (MSC) chaired by David, now Lord Young. He came from a group of modernist Tories who believed in utilitarian education and the need to make schooling more vocational.

While educationists initially detested the MSC, it in its turn characterised the Education Department as having little or no influence on schools while the MSC had both power and money. This early and widespread criticism of the department was an important factor in determining how its ministers and civil servants would exercise the considerable powers given to them by the 1988 Education Reform Act.

There is no doubt that the MSC initiative and the introduction of the GCSE were extremely beneficial to state schools, changing teaching methods and attitudes in secondary education more than almost anything else had done. There are arguments about whether we – while our competitors do not – need an examination at 16, but there is no doubt that GCSE coursework and the changes it brought to teaching methods motivated less able youngsters in a way that the previous examination system had not.

With all these changes, it can be argued that many of the 1988 reforms were already in place without some of the prescription and detail which was to plague the introduction of the national curriculum. There is, therefore, a valid case for saying that in 1988 the need for a national curriculum was less urgent than it had been in the early 1980s.

All these arguments were obscured by a crescendo of complaints from industry and the far right of the Tory party which were fuelled by the more extreme behaviour of some educationists, who were unable or unwilling to compromise. Attitudes of politicians and parents were changing too quickly for them and some were determined to fight a rearguard action to combat the reaction they could see was inevitable. More of them, however, did not notice what was happening. This group was so insular that it simply took the grand view that politicians should not interfere in education, and neither should the public. It was the classic case, which has infuriated so many parents down the ages, of teachers knowing best when quite clearly they did not. Even if they did, nobody now was disposed to believe them.

It was around this time that Mrs Thatcher became involved, gathering around her a number of far-right educationists who wanted a return to what has become called traditional teaching, the same people who were talking of a return to Victorian values.

Keith Joseph, her education secretary, was attracted by the arguments, looking back at his own classical education with fond memories. He was also a monetarist and was aware that traditional teaching was cheaper and might even act as a brake on the rising cost of maintaining the state education service. He certainly was not into spending any more money and knew that modern methods and a lower pupil–teacher ratio would mean extra spending. He was an extremely complex man, passionately concerned about vocational education and the failure of the system to provide properly for the lower 40 per cent of the country's children. He was genuinely concerned about the disadvantaged and found himself in a difficult position with some of his cabinet colleagues, which probably explains why he became so indecisive in his last years in government.

Joseph appeared to be visibly torn between the constraints of monetarism and the need to invest in education. I remember at the end of a day visiting Suffolk schools which had amply demonstrated that excellent schools could go no further in the face of the next round of cuts, standing alone with Sir Keith on a snow-swept platform at Ipswich station. After a formal farewell, he impulsively grabbed me by the shoulders and said: "I leave you a sadder but a wiser man." A long sigh, a shake of the head, and off into the night. Nothing changed. Like many others, I have retained a lasting affection for the man. He was certainly not part of the inexorable move to a national curriculum. His heart lay with Margaret Thatcher and her group who took a simplistic view of education and set the Conservatives on the path of government by prejudice.

The right-wing of the Conservative party was listening to lobbyists who were continually ringing their hands, saying how terrible it was that none of the country's children – apart from their own – could read or write, and that something had to be done, without having the slightest idea what it was that had to be done, or how intractable the problems were.

My theory is that somebody, either in government or in the Education Department, decided to head off that group from leading state education to total disaster by inventing the national curriculum which appeared to satisfy a lot of their demands. The accent was on rigour. From that moment on nobody concerned with government education policy has dared utter a sentence that did not contain the word. The argument for rigour and standards was irrefutable if there was a genuine desire to provide a good education for all our children, to ensure that they received the broad and balanced schooling to which they were all entitled.

Once the extreme right wing was blocked, the battleground shifted to an argument about how many subjects should be compulsory. Mrs Thatcher was in favour of the three-subject curriculum of mathematics, English and science. Kenneth Baker, who had replaced Joseph as Secretary of State for Education in May 1986, was quite determined not to be saddled with anything that was so right wing, so nihilistic and negative, and argued successfully for the more respectable broader ten-subject curriculum.

6

The government's task then was to set up individual working groups for each subject. That is where I first encountered the national curriculum to be enshrined in the government's 1988 Education Reform Act. The national curriculum was the core around which all the other reforms were built as part of the government's aim to increase parental choice by giving them more information about schools and their performance, settling more powers on schools to manage their own affairs, even to the point of allowing them to opt-out of local authority control and to be financed directly by central government.

And I entered all that by accident. I had become reasonably well known to ministers and the Civil Service largely because I had been a member of the Burnham Committee through all the pay negotiations and was seen as a good negotiator. The Burnham Committee set up a number of working groups in 1984 to look at teachers' conditions of service and, as nobody was interested in appraisal, I was asked to chair the appraisal committee.

The Education Department funded a pilot scheme in Suffolk which led to the National Steering Group which I chaired until 1988. This inevitably brought me into contact with ministers and civil servants, but then in 1987 I opted out of education and moved to Humberside County Council, the first education officer to become chief executive of a major county. It was not long, however, before I was back in the fray following an invitation from HMI to join the government's mathematics working group.

Such invitations are never explained. I was certainly not a mathematician and may simply have been selected as the statutory chief education officer, although I was no longer even that. This, however, was also at the time when it had become clear that Conservative politicians, including Kenneth Baker, were deeply suspicious of the education professionals and were well aware that groups of experts set up to consider a specific subject could get out of hand. It could be, therefore, that the Education Department had decided that it would be good to have somebody with a broad perspective.

I did not meet Baker until December 1987 when he appointed me chairman of the mathematics working group following the resignation of the original chairman. I found a man who was an unreserved convert to the national curriculum. I was struck by his sense of purpose, by the fact that he was determined to achieve genuine curriculum changes and realistic rigour to drive up standards. Amidst all the bombast claiming that this was the biggest ever education reform, he genuinely believed it could change British education for the better and that he had rescued it from the worst. I would not have agreed to be chairman of the mathematics working group if that had not been the case. I saw him two or three times during the next six months to give him progress reports and came to know him. When the mathematics report was finally finished but not yet published we had a long meeting when he indicated that he was aware that I was having some difficulties in Humberside, partly because of the time I was spending away from the county but also because some councillors did not approve of the idea of the working group.

There had been no detailed plans for how the newly created National Curriculum Council would operate but I, like other people, had assumed that it would have a chairman and a chief executive. Looking back, I think Baker may have been exploring the possibility of making me chairman but ruled it out because he knew that I could not combine it with my role as chief executive of a major authority. He suggested that I might be better out of Humberside and I remember wondering what on earth he was talking about.

The county council had 36 Labour, 36 Tories and 4 Liberals, 44,000 staff and a £600 million budget, and I had been there for only a year. Riding that tiger and getting the mathematics document written was more than enough to keep me from worrying too much about a future elsewhere so my thinking was not taking me where Baker's was going. The day before the May meeting of the county council, his private secretary rang to ask me to have lunch with Baker the following day but I declined because of the county council meeting. I remember being totally uninterested at that point in anything connected with the national curriculum, let alone any thoughts of a job. The official said it was extremely urgent, but I was unimpressed. He then telephoned back to ask if I could possibly attend an evening meeting with Mr Baker the day after that of the county council. There was clearly some urgency in their eyes but I was still not thinking along their lines. I agreed to go but it was a standing joke with the Civil Service that I had cavalierly told the Secretary of State that I was too busy to have lunch with him at a critical time for the future of state education.

I went in the train to London knowing that there must be something interesting in the wind but having no idea what it could be. I was put in the ante-room outside his office at the Department of Education and Science and into the room came Jenny Bacon, one of the senior civil servants responsible for the curriculum. Surprised that I did not know precisely why I had been called down, she told me that the government had created the combined post of chairman and chief executive and that it was going to be offered to me. She gave me a document of five or six pages which was a very glorified – if unreal – job specification.

The document had been prepared because, I learned later, there was enormous difficulty with the Treasury in getting the job uprated to a salary that would be attractive to me. The document was far from clear because the Treasury and the civil servants did not want a National Curriculum Council, still less did they want somebody who was highly ranked running it. They were going to find out that nothing less than deputy secretary level would do.

8

The pros and cons of taking the job went through my mind in the fifteen minutes or so that I was waiting to see Baker, surrounded by pictures of his twenty-one predecessors including Margaret Thatcher, the only one of them to go on to be prime minister. Then in a rush I was whistled into the Secretary of State's room to find Sir David Hancock, the permanent secretary, and Nick Stuart, a deputy secretary, with Baker who was smiling from ear to ear. He greeted me like an old friend and produced a malt whisky before anything was said. We sat down in the armchairs in the corner of his barn of an office in the old DES headquarters in Elizabeth House in Waterloo.

Baker said he knew I had been told why I had been called down and that he would like to offer me the job of chairman and chief executive of the National Curriculum Council because I had shown that I was a 'can do' man by delivering the mathematics working group report on time. He was full of praise about that and said that what he was offering was possibly the most important job in education and certainly one of the most influential.

Baker understood that the only way for me to be given an acceptable salary and a full-time job was to combine the two posts of chairman and chief executive. The public reason, and it was a perfectly proper one, was that one person had to take on the task to drive the curriculum through but we both agreed that was something which would have to be reviewed in due course. He then gave me a personal vision of what he wanted. He was determined that the national curriculum would make a quality education available for all our children. If I had any doubts, it was his enthusiasm and commitment that really sold the job to me. He also outlined the problems which the National Curriculum Council faced, such as the professional sensibilities of teachers, for example. There was, he said, an enormous ambassadorial job to be done in selling the national curriculum to teachers and parents. He did not refer at all to the right wing and any problems he might be having within his own group. He knew he was having problems, I knew he was having problems, but we did not talk about them as all of that was understood between us.

That meeting was a commentary on both of us: it was gloriously unspecific. He offered me a concept of what the job was even if the details were decidedly vague. He sought my help and I gave it gladly. The job seemed interesting and by any measure would be difficult to turn down. It was a national job that appealed to my sense of duty and sense of excitement. Above all I realised by then that the national curriculum was in danger of going out of control if somebody did not get a grip of it and I believed that I had some chance of doing that.

I left that night very buoyed up, very impressed by Baker's idealism, his sense of purpose and vision and his realism about the problems that had to be tackled. I was also flattered by his faith in me. The offer was irresistible provided the logistical problems could be solved, such as the conditions of service and salary, how quickly I could leave Humberside, and the crucial question of where NCC would be based as I was not keen on moving to London. In the event, I was given a seven-year contract for procedural and legal reasons but left the impression with Baker that I would not be there for more than three to five years and would not want to be.

The aims were clear but there was plenty that could still go wrong. There was no National Curriculum Council, there was no building, the Education Reform Act had not been passed and would not be passed until 18 August, and the reports of the mathematics and science working groups were still to be published.

On the way back to Humberside I began to realise that the scope and intensity of the national curriculum would undoubtedly lead to difficulties. It was obvious to me even then that the subject by subject approach and the detail contained within each subject would inevitably lead to conflict between the various subjects and put pressure on the curriculum if other subjects were to be added. Nevertheless, I believed then and still believe that the country needed a national curriculum and that there was enough in the Education Reform Act to make state education very much better than anything that had gone before; that it would set and raise standards in schools across the country without imposing dull conformity. For his part, Baker had enough belief in the national curriculum to make it work at crucial times, forcing through the changes that mattered. I believe, too, that whatever happened thereafter he would have been prepared to stay on and see it through.

The night I was appointed I told Baker that the site of the headquarters would have to be of my choosing. The civil servants agreed that there was no absolute necessity for NCC to be based in London, a view they came to regret, and Baker indicated that subject to Treasury approval he would have no objection.

The reasons for choosing York were partly personal, but I was also beginning to have the first glimmer of what it was going to be like to live with the civil servants who became involved in the strong lobby for joint London offices for the National Curriculum Council and the School Examinations and Assessment Council (SEAC). As it turned out, nobody whom we worked with in SEAC or in the Civil Service were worried about York. They were all happy to escape from London, while the council's own staff had chosen to be there.

The one group that was never happy was that comprised of the members who lived in London, and that was most of them. They would have preferred meetings near their homes and there was always pressure to hold meetings in the capital, which I resisted. Once the members became unsettled and difficult towards the end of my time at NCC it was those who lived in London who did the most complaining.

Whatever the criticisms might be, the National Curriculum Council and its staff got the job done. When he appointed me, Baker had also said that I would have to drive NCC, that if it came to the crunch I would have to make the decisions and that the members would have to follow. That was probably the root cause of later trouble.

Sadly, perhaps for good reasons, some members of the council never really understood the pace and pressure for change imposed by the imperatives of the government. Because most of them were educational professionals, they did not fully understand the demands made by Baker and the requirements of the law for rapid and permanent change. They sometimes wanted to take a paper back for three months or complained with some justification that all the decisions were being taken by the officers when they wanted to make up their own minds. Too often, when given the chance, some would not make up their minds while others would not have had time to read vital papers before meetings. They did, however, have some valid things to say. We were being forced along at an unreasonable pace and some pressures from ministers and officials should have been resisted. Increasingly I found myself in the cruel position of being pulled both ways. Maybe I should have joined dissidents on NCC and told ministers that we were not going to play ball, but I think that would have brought even greater problems.

2

THE CIVIL SERVANTS DESCEND

When I agreed to run the National Curriculum Council, I thought, as it proved naïvely, that the Civil Service and NCC would be allies in the joint task of delivering the national curriculum. There were vital things that I did not know.

One was that NCC and School Examinations and Assessment Council (SEAC) had been created against the advice and wishes of the civil servants who had been successful in limiting the powers of both bodies. NCC was very strongly advisory as distinct from executive. Kenneth Baker believed that it had wide executive powers; the civil servants did not, and unfortunately they were right. My understanding was that the council would have the power to do certain things on its own account but in the end even this limited power proved illusory. Kenneth Baker told me that he saw the council as a source of professional advice to balance against that of officials from the Department of Education and Science (DES). If so, this would not be music to the ears of civil servants.

All the evidence suggests that they did not want the National Curriculum Council because they wanted to run the curriculum themselves with some help from what would effectively become a subordinate HMI. Baker made it clear to me on more than one occasion that the politicians had to fight the Civil Service to create NCC and SEAC. He therefore put me on my guard.

The creation of the National Curriculum Council brought to an end the brief existence of the School Curriculum Development Committee (SCDC), a London-based body with 40 or 50 staff, who as a group, while undoubtedly talented, were light years away from the hard rigour of delivering a national curriculum.

The whole idea of the working groups and the National Curriculum Council was absolutely different from anything that any education professionals had experienced before. The Education Act reforms were not born of these people, they were not consulted about them, indeed the

12

government considered them to be the enemy. In that sense it was a brutal business, mitigated only by the realisation of some senior civil servants that in the end the partnership between the professionals and the council would have to be restored.

Even when they became deeply involved in the national curriculum with all its pressures and deadlines, some members of the education profession still did not realise the enormity of the change. It was also a shock to me, but having spent a lifetime in local and national politics I came fairly early on to realise that what was happening was a radical shift in educational power and the way in which schools were to be run in the future.

There was also a marked change in the attitude of civil servants after the introduction of the 1988 Education Reform Act, which they rightly saw as their first chance of having real power over state education. There was a volatile mixture of palpable fear of failing to deliver what was expected of them and a determination to run the whole programme. This was the first time ever that the DES had control of the curriculum and it was the beginning of the demise of HMI, although that was barely appreciated at the time. The fear of officials may well have come from being in the front line as never before.

Meanwhile, I was having to work with staff from the SCDC which, as an organisation, was philosophically opposed to everything the national curriculum stood for. The hostility was open. The committee had paid little attention to the national curriculum. An honourable exception was the acting chief executive Peter Watkins who was the first to recognise both the strengths and weaknesses inherent in the national curriculum.

Staff at the SCDC were working on a whole range of documents and working groups, and long after I arrived continued to write aggressively non-national curriculum documents even though they had lived under its shadow for a year. They made no concessions and had even commissioned a paper on primary mathematics that made no mention of the national curriculum despite the fact that the working group report had been published

The thought that the council was not going to be in London raised the temperature by a thousand degrees. The staff were faced either with leaving with a modest severance package or coming to the National Curriculum Council in York. They were philosophically opposed, they were York opposed, and they were patronised by the civil servants, some of whom treated them rather shabbily.

The Schools Council (SC) that the SCDC had partially replaced had a big bureaucracy and was a partnership with local government which was anathema to the Conservatives. Once the SC was abolished it was clear that never again would there be a body that got in the way of civil servants, which threatened ministers, or gave any kind of voice to local government. Above all nobody ever again was to control both the curriculum and examinations, a determination that led to the eventual decision to set up NCC and SEAC as two quite separate bodies. SCDC was, therefore, created to be as woolly and advisory as possible. The real powers of the Schools Council were largely translated into the School Examination Council which with the passing of the 1988 Act became the School Examinations and Assessment Council, with extended powers to cover the newly introduced testing of children at 7, 11, and 14. Accordingly, SEAC tended to be a traditional body moving on with its established staff and difficult to change, which created some tensions with NCC, a largely new organisation with only a few enterprising souls who braved the journey north to give some continuity. The tradition of NCC would have to grow: virtually nothing was inherited.

In setting up NCC and in appointing me, Baker had stressed that the independence of the council was vital. The civil servants, however, had decided that was not going to be the case and that both the council and its officials were in effect going to do as they were told, although they would have expressed this more elegantly. The relationship between NCC and ministers was largely good until the advent of Kenneth Clarke, and to a lesser extent, the two junior ministers, Tim Eggar and Michael Fallon – but their role in the story comes much later.

In the Baker and MacGregor eras it was always difficult to know when the civil servants were acting on behalf of their political masters and when they were acting on their own account. There is no doubt that when it came to insisting that reports were workable and ready on time they were acting on behalf of ministers. Neither Baker nor MacGregor could contemplate the slightest delay. They were both concerned that any postponement in the early stages could allow the professionals in education to fight back or that it would give the oppportunity for their own right wing to intervene. There might not even be a national curriculum if it was allowed to wither on the vine of delay and procrastination.

While Baker and MacGregor were in control I never once failed to touch base with a politician although it often appeared that attempts were made to prevent me getting to them in the first place. Once we met, however, I always succeeded in coming away with agreement on the lines that the council favoured.

Another thing I did not know was that the Civil Service as a whole had a decided distaste for quangos. They see them as bad news, difficult to control and, more importantly, as taking power from the Civil Service. There is what amounts to a standard textbook way of sorting them out which was applied to NCC from the start: strangle the budget, amend or delay the corporate plan, interfere at meetings.

Civil servants, perhaps due to their own experience, find it difficult either to accept or understand that once politicians set up committees the people appointed are not quasi-civil servants, and are not susceptible to discipline. Lay members, particularly if personally appointed by the Secretary of State as was the case with NCC, could reasonably expect to be entitled to express their own views which are likely to be as valid as those of the civil servants. They also knew that they had to work within the constraints of what ministers would wear, and that confrontation was in nobody's interest.

I was not involved in selecting members of the council. Kenneth Baker interviewed the candidates himself. They were his personal choice: following the bad experience of the original mathematics working group, which will be dealt with in the following chapter, he was no longer prepared to take the risk of accepting lists of names offered by officials. He was determined to make the selection himself from a much wider choice. Nevertheless, the members of that first group were largely educational professionals and were not, on the whole, political appointments. The first council meeting did not have a political feel except that all the members had indicated that they were in favour of a national curriculum. They subscribed to the general philosophy but did not come as political nominees as was to happen later on. There was no suggestion at that time of any of them reporting back to ministers or of them being in inner circles. The education profession had very little to complain about.

The council set off with good will all round, coupled with a fair degree of bewilderment about what was expected. The first meeting of what was then a shadow council took place in York in July 1988 before the Act had been passed. There was a great deal of confusion among members as to why they were there as they had received very little briefing from either ministers or officials on their role; optimism, though, was high. Most of them had not met each other – I had only met one of them before – but we all received our first warning from the civil servants in the form of a lecture on good behaviour which shook some of us, even though it was not the heavy hand we were to experience later and gave no more than a clue as to how tied the council was going to be. I sometimes wondered if certain of the senior officials had ever previously attended a democratic committee.

Civil servants were recorded on the minutes as observers, but they were far more than that. Sometimes they would come in packs. They were at every meeting of the council, working groups, and committees. They spoke at every meeting, frequently upsetting the council with what some saw as arrogance and a dictatorial manner if they believed somebody was stepping out of line. In fairness, this was as much due to their lack of experience as anything else. A month or two in a local education office would have done them no harm. The best of the civil servants adapted quickly.

I had no objection to them being there as assessors but did object to them attempting to take over. Before the National Curriculum Council I had never been to a meeting where members of committees often felt

15

outnumbered by the assessors and observers. Members of the council did once decide to rebel and say that only two officials could attend a meeting: they complained that they were surrounded by them. What the council failed to get right was the balance between hearing the Secretary of State's views, and being able, with due regard to those views, to make its own decisions.

From the very first moment I was told that all the papers for our meetings should go to the Education Department officials a fortnight beforehand for their views. We had constitutional crisis after constitutional crisis about their right to see the papers. The council compromised by allowing them to comment on the papers but not to alter them. As a result, every draft paper would be sent to up to six different civil servants to be returned, usually late, with about twenty suggested amendments, some of them rather abrupt and frequently contradictory. The council officers were therefore left doing the paper their way, knowing that at the meeting where it was presented the civil servants would preface their objections by saying that they had already expressed their reservations to the chief executive. They consistently took the line that nothing should be considered by the council that they had not seen and, by implication, approved. This put pressure both on members and their officers.

It was made perfectly clear by education department officials that they would expect to see and approve everything that went to the Secretary of State, from a formal submission on consultation documents to a brief letter of advice. If not, they implied that the proposal would be thrown out. Conform to their advice and plain sailing. Stick to your guns and have hostile views passed on to ministers. Catch 22!

This was, of course, partly due to the way the system of government works in this country but it does show how easily so-called independent advice can be manipulated. The attempts to make sure that the consultation documents said exactly what the civil servants wanted them to say as distinct from what NCC wanted them to say in aggregate made the advice to NCC little more than a set of instructions. Sometimes the council knuckled under and sometimes it did not. More often than not it did.

Members of the first council deserve a great deal of praise for the courage with which they fought their corner. The quality of their thinking and of debate was high and deserved to be taken more seriously.

Having gained a measure of control of the council's papers, the Education Department then set out to control the budget which was used quite cynically to keep the council in its place: the council should tell them what it wanted to do and then they would say whether there was any money available. When it came to day-to-day control the council found that it had to go cap in hand to the Education Department for permission to spend its own money. The fact that the council's finance staff were professional and entrepreneurial did not seem to help. The government was preaching enterprise and commercial approaches: these did not percolate through the layers of Treasury and departmental bureaucracy.

Control of the budget was also used to determine the shape of the contents of the corporate plan. The council was told from the beginning that there would have to be a five-year plan, but when it drew up its rolling programme based on what it thought it had to do it ran straight into a brick wall. It was doubted whether the Secretary of State would sanction money to be spent on anything that was not directly connected with the introduction of the ten subjects. It seemed like a game – you work out rationally what you want to do and we will tell you why you can't.

Council meetings and major committees were usually attended by a deputy secretary and Eric Bolton, the then Senior Chief HMI, who did not see himself as part of the Civil Service and was fighting his own battle to regain curriculum control for HMI. Meanwhile, many of his inspectors carried on as if nothing had changed, running courses on the national curriculum, producing their own documents, and holding meetings.

The council took the line that if there were meetings on the national curriculum then they should at least be run in conjunction with its officers. Some inspectors, however, took the view that they were not to be displaced and found it very hard to co-operate with the council. That was to change totally, but not until needless confusion and tension had made life difficult all round.

All of this was very upsetting for NCC's professional staff who would find themselves on the same platform as HMI with different briefs, with the implication that NCC did not know what they were talking about. Apart from providing ammunition for people anxious to cause trouble it spread a very damaging message of confusion. It also indicated that some members of HMI were inherently hostile to the very idea of a national curriculum. HMI continually stressed their independence and we were told early on that HMI considered they had a right to inspect the National Curriculum Council.

Once there was a large number of committees the Education Department had to send lower level officials who were often ill-informed on the implications of the work. Many of these junior officials did not understand the problems, had not been properly briefed, had no concept of how to handle committees, and at times wrote reports that were misleading. This did not inhibit them from frequently laying down the law to far better qualified people, leaving staff and members distraught and angry. Some of them became quite well known for their own hobby-horses, which they rode quite shamelessly.

Junior officials would come to NCC meetings to tell a group of teachers how, for example, geography should be taught. This did damage as the teachers reported back to their schools, adding fuel to the argument that the council was not independent. Protestations of independence were rejected, which was hardly surprising as the council was being constantly undermined by the very people who should have been there to support it. When the council was revising the English report, for example, dealing with the place of grammar in the curriculum, one junior official instructed members to do certain things because 'the minister required it'. They often used the word 'minister' when they meant their own senior official and when they said that the minister would not be happy with one of our proposals one could be fairly sure that the minister had never been consulted, or that he had displayed an unlikely and encyclopaedic grasp of detail.

The civil servants appeared to be governed by a mixture of mistrust of the council and a fear of upsetting ministers to whom they took every minute detail. Judging the influence of the civil servants and whether or not they were speaking for ministers has to be qualified by the knowledge that it is quite possible they were being used by the politicians. Without being in the same room as the politicians and civil servants it is impossible to know. The versions which emerge after such meetings have to be interpreted with consummate care.

Officials, however, were in and out every day giving their view of events, and therefore people in my position often did not hear at first hand what was required and were well down the line in terms of influence. This was not a question of being in York or in London but of hour by hour contact. Philip Halsey, the chief executive and chairman of SEAC based in London and a former senior civil servant, felt that he faced the same difficulties. Had we had a genuine rapport with officials we would have known what the Secretary of State wanted, we would have known what our councils would or would not deliver, and we could have found the best way forward. Both Halsey and myself had expected a degree of trust and sharing of information which did not materialise. Had it done so things might have gone more productively.

There were often things which council members wanted to do which were beyond their powers, but the way round this was to let people have their say before steering the debate to the required conclusion. The Civil Service approach tended to be counter-productive and self-defeating. Members were too often left feeling unnecessarily resentful. Some of their best ideas only demonstrated how inflexible a government machine was if it could not cope – in such a situation nothing is more at risk than a good idea.

The clear message given to members of the council – all of them appointed by the Secretary of State – was that they were there to rubber-stamp papers and minutes that had been written in a way which best represented the views of the DES, or were, in the eyes of the department, most acceptable to ministers.

Education Department officials wrote separate minutes for ministers and we sometimes wondered whether ours ever got through to them or whether they simply read briefing papers prepared by the civil servants which were not always an objective account of our views. As a result, I would sometimes find that when we did meet ministers we were working from quite different pieces of paper.

During the first six months of NCC I found myself being kept away from ministers although I had been led to believe by Kenneth Baker – and I am sure he meant it – that I would see him quite frequently and that he would seek my views on a wide range of issues. It soon became clear that, far from seeing Baker regularly, I was only going to be brought before him on stage-managed occasions and that it was a clear policy decision, probably taken without his knowledge, as Philip Halsey was facing the same problems. The council became restive because they assumed that they too would be seeing Baker more regularly but all we had was a single visit, fine as far as it went but not leading to a good working relationship.

While described by some people outside the council as the man in charge of the curriculum I was in reality a prisoner of the system, trapped between a council which was beginning to believe that it was being side-lined and a Civil Service able to organise events to meet its own ambitions. Meetings with the Secretary of State were attended by up to twelve officials who, working together, would brief him beforehand so that the cards were always stacked against the council. It took a perceptive minister to see through the stage-management. To his credit, Baker often did.

Officials from the Education Department always behaved perfectly when in the presence of ministers but there was little opportunity to express any disquiet. It says something about modern government that journalists have more opportunity for private conversations with ministers than those appointed to work with them.

The situation reached crisis level in the spring of 1989 when the council set out to address the problem of what came to be known as the whole curriculum, a phrase that became politically unacceptable. The legally required curriculum, together with the preamble of the Act insisting on breadth and balance, raised simple questions: what is the moral justification for all this, what is education about, what is the whole curriculum into which this fits? The whole curriculum would include subjects such as the classics, economics, business studies, as well as personal and social education, health and careers.

All of this interested a great number of people. Many teachers did not like the ten subject limit and feared they were being railroaded into a narrow and mechanistic curriculum. Industrialists were also very suspicious. They wanted schools to produce rounded literate and numerate individuals prepared for the world of work. If NCC was to become a body of national repute it would have to offer clear guidance without cutting back on the work on the compulsory curriculum, a view, however, not shared by ministers and civil servants.

The council was told that its job was to deliver the ten national curriculum subjects: everything else could be dealt with once the original brief was achieved. Civil servants said ministers believed that work on the whole curriculum could result in a major distraction that might allow the establishment to fight back. The majority of council members wanted to look at the whole curriculum and it was not long before they decided to set up a whole curriculum committee, against the specific advice of civil servants who felt that the council was moving into areas that were not our concern. The council was straight into the first major quandary.

Baker was clearly concerned that the Whole Curriculum Committee (WCC) could prove to be a distraction that he could do without. He did not, though, appear to be worried about the idea itself. The committee took on a number of outside people, became quite ambitious, and was in danger of fulfilling Baker's fears, but did publish guidance setting out how the national curriculum could fit in with additional subjects at 14 and the other elements that should permeate the education of every child, such as an awareness of multicultural needs, equal opportunities, and disability.

All of these were very softly stated but the council did list five themes it thought were essential to all education: citizenship, environment, economic and industrial understanding, careers, and health. The council also announced that it proposed to publish guidance on each of them and set up working groups which included representatives from industry. Each guidance booklet would be a compendium of good practice although not, of course, statutory. None of this could be described as contentious and could have been used within the ten subjects or as separate lessons, depending on the wishes of individual schools.

Then the roof fell in. A posse of civil servants descended on York to tell NCC that it could not continue work on nor publish the five booklets. They were a dangerous distraction, funds were not available, and work would have to be delayed until 1993 when the national curriculum was due to be fully implemented.

Clearly alarmed by what he had been told by the civil servants, Kenneth Baker wrote a detailed two-page letter to the council in May 1989 in which he told it to abandon investigations into the whole curriculum and get on with the real work of introducing the curriculum. In the future nothing should go to formal meetings of the council for approval until it had been seen and approved by the Secretary of State. Here was the question of independence in a nutshell. There was something that did not add up: industry was in favour of our whole curriculum approach and had representatives on the working groups. Baker was friendly with industry and yet he appeared to want to stop work which they approved and supported.

At that point I decided that I had to see Baker and telephoned him at home. I was well received. He asked how the council was getting on, showed some surprise that we had not seen each other more often, and asked what the problem was. I told him bluntly that he had signed a letter which would have had electric consequences on the future of the council and would lead to him parting company with his industrial friends who wanted a rounded curriculum. I also stated that I wanted to be perfectly sure he fully appreciated what was happening. He showed great concern and said that we should meet urgently without civil servants. His first available date was 16 June in Betws-y-Coed, North Wales, where he was staying overnight before going on to do a half marathon for charity the following morning. As it happened I was in Wales that weekend for a meeting of the Curriculum Council for Wales so we both had perfect cover.

A helicopter was waiting for Baker in a field behind the hotel. I went with some trepidation as I wondered whom he would have with him. Dressed in his running gear, he came out of the hotel alone to meet me and shook me warmly by the hand. We went into the hotel and found a room where we talked over coffee. We started with the letter and its implications. He looked at it and could not believe he had signed it. It was one of those magic moments in life. We then discussed whether he really wanted the publicity that would follow the sudden cancellation of the working groups. He asked why I thought the civil servants had advised him so strongly and accepted that he had been persuaded by the argument that work of this sort could prove to be a distraction. He accepted the council's argument that if it did not give advice and guidance there would be even more distraction as schools would spend time making up their own curriculum. He accepted too that it was a question of personal trust and that he trusted me to ensure that if the working groups continued, the main thrust of the council's work would continue to be the introduction of the national curriculum.

Still talking, we walked out to the helicopter. He said he was very shaken and angry by what had happened and that we should meet more regularly, whereupon he climbed into the helicopter to be whisked off to the start of his half marathon. The letter was never withdrawn, I undertook not to make it an issue and at NCC's next meeting a senior civil servant made a speech stressing the council's independence. Cynics might believe that in the same way as football managers are given a vote of confidence before being sacked, the council ceased to have any real importance once it had been assured of its independence.

Nevertheless, the working groups published their reports, which are now in use in nearly every school. The work in these areas is strong and it has not diminished the national curriculum: it has enhanced it. The overall plan was that the five separate documents would be put into an omnibus version setting out the values and attitudes that should underpin the entire curriculum, in a restatement of the whole curriculum. This would also allow the addition of material on multicultural education and equal opportunities which are not adequately covered in the work done so far by NCC. This was one of the first things to be stopped when I left the council.

The meeting in Wales reaffirmed NCC's right to have direct access to Baker but there were still considerable difficulties: if I said I wanted to see the Secretary of State on my own, a hundred alarm bells would ring and by the autumn there had been very little improvement. Civil Service pressure was still causing trouble, so I approached Sir David Hancock, the permanent secretary. To my great joy he took me to the Athenaeum in Pall Mall for lunch where he listened to everything I said. He was discreet enough not to be critical of his officials but from that moment on, whilst he was there, I had access to Baker. That meeting was a turning point and relations improved so that by the end of my time at NCC the civil servants had backed off. In retrospect, I should probably have approached Sir David earlier. I was learning to assume nothing about the Whitehall system.

The seeds of the problems that I ultimately faced were, however, sowed by these distracting and debilitating power struggles. Having worked for political masters of all colours it becomes clear what is and is not acceptable. There is no point, for example, in selling a Labour administration a return to grammar schools or proposing to Kenneth Baker anything that was against the policies of the Conservative Government.

There was never anything that NCC wanted to do that would have embarrassed Baker. Members were aware of the constraints but believed they could offer valuable independent advice within those constraints. The difficulties in the beginning were not, therefore, primarily political, but lay in the growing belief of some in the Education Department that they knew best what should be in the curriculum even though they had never taught or been near a state school. The failures of some educational professionals had given them an opportunity. Now they too were in the front line – and the firing line.

3

WHEN TWO AND TWO DIDN'T MAKE FOUR

The telephone call that was to lead me finally to the National Curriculum Council came in the summer of 1987 to my office in Beverley not long after I had been appointed chief executive of Humberside County Council. The call was from one of Her Majesty's Inspectors of schools to ask whether I would serve on the mathematics working group being formed by Kenneth Baker, the Secretary of State for Education. The group would set out what every 5- to 16-year-old in every state school in England and Wales should know about mathematics, one of the ten compulsory subjects in the proposed new national curriculum.

I am not a mathematician and knew very little about the as yet unwritten national curriculum. Engrossed in the problems of Humberside, it had passed me by. I was only dimly aware of the ten subjects and I knew that mathematics and science were going to be the first. What I did not appreciate any more than anyone else at the beginning was that this was a highly political exercise, to be played to a new set of rules.

Many of the later troubles which dogged the introduction of the curriculum stemmed from the fact that nobody realised the enormity of the task being undertaken. Baker was asking all those involved to undertake, within a year, one of the most dramatic rethinks in British state education, and that in the area of the curriculum where central government had by tradition avoided direct intervention.

In the past the Education Department would have set up a committee to consider a specific subject or area of education and asked for its recommendations in due course. Such a committee would frequently sit for two years or more, perhaps to decide in the end that the proposition it was considering was not feasible or that no changes in the *status quo* were required. Baker was going to have none of that: unfortunately the people appointed to the first working groups were unaware of the change of atmosphere in British education. The government was going to insist that the job was done and that for the most part it was done the government's way. The culture shock was too much for some of the working group members who were used to the more genteel committee work of an era that Kenneth Baker had turned his back on.

The proposal was revolutionary in the sense that the remit of the working group was that it would be required within a matter of only a few months to determine what society would, in this particular case, expect a child to know in mathematics at 7, 11, 14, and 16. Its recommendations would form the basis of the national curriculum in mathematics to be taught in 24,000 state schools in England and Wales and would come to be generally accepted by the country's 1,400 independent schools.

The public at large, and some educationists and teachers in particular, still do not realise how dramatically different this was from the kind of working groups and committees of inquiry that educational professionals had been asked to join in the past. The new role that the mathematics working group and the science working group members were being asked to play was certainly challenging; it was also very frightening. What I see in retrospect is that the civil servants and HMI had chosen a working group of 15 or 17 people who could be expected to deliver the traditional style report. They were used to making a series of recommendations and to advocating a few improvements in teaching methods only to see the report get lost, ignored or emasculated by the government that had set it up. I am quite sure that the members of the mathematics working group did not realise precisely what it was that they were being asked to do. I certainly did not.

In any event, the group was not geared to producing, in the face of the palpable distrust of everybody else in education, something which was going to be imposed on every state school in education whether the profession approved or not. Baker expected the reports of all the working groups to be hard and tough, to use unfamiliar words such as 'rigour' and 'delivery', and that they would be backed by the government and enshrined in law. And it all had to be done within a year. Announcing the appointment and role of the working groups earlier in the year, Kenneth Baker had made it all sound so simple. He told the education, science, and arts Select Committee:

> The government wants the national curriculum to be as good as the best minds in the country can make it. The level of attainment to be aimed at and the content of what is taught should reflect the best practice of our good schools. The duties placed on the schools should leave full scope for good teaching and for this country's tradition that teachers use their professional talents and skills to adapt the work to each pupil and to develop new approaches as the new needs arise.

The sting was in the tail:

> Two aspects of our educational tradition will have to be modified. First, we can no longer leave individual teachers, schools or local education authorities, to decide the curriculum children should follow. It is no longer acceptable that many children have a much less good curriculum than others through the accident of where they happen to go to school.

Baker also offered a definition of how the curriculum would be structured. He said that it would be necessary for each subject within the foundation curriculum, the ten subjects of mathematics, English, science, technology, modern languages, history, geography, art, music, and physical education, to have clear and challenging attainment targets for the key ages of 7, 11, and 14 which later came to be known as the key stages, KS1, KS2, and KS3. At that point the can of worms that was to become key stage 4 had not even been spotted on the shelf.

Baker told the Commons committee:

> These targets should allow for variations in ability. They should not result in an unduly narrow approach to teaching and learning. Having established the attainment targets it will be necesary to determine and define the essential content, skills and processes of what has to be covered and taught in each subject.

The task of the science and mathematics working groups may have been clear in Baker's eyes: it was never explained to me precisely what the groups would be expected to do. When I joined the other members at their second meeting in August 1987 they were already in considerable difficulty. Civil servants had explained that each national curriculum subject would consist of a number of attainment targets for children at different ages which would be supported by programmes of study, setting out what children should be taught in order to reach those targets. Members of the groups, however, including myself, were still unclear precisely what either of these were or what the concepts meant. How did a programme of study differ from a scheme of work? How many attainment targets was a group to aim at: two or 200, five or 500? Later it was made clear that profile components would group a number of attainment targets together under a central theme, such as knowledge and understanding, and could be weighted to give one more importance than another. How was this to be arrived at?

Like me, the majority of the working group had been chosen on the advice of HMI rather than the DES civil servants and this I believe was the cause of later difficulties, as the officials surely must have known exactly what would be required while the inspectors perhaps did not. These difficulties led to acrimonious exchanges between Baker and the civil servants over the membership of the mathematics working group and the science working group. He appeared to believe that there had been a conspiracy between the Education Department and HMI to choose people they knew would inevitably thwart ministers. The charge was unfair. If the selection of members was inappropriate it was because nobody had realised that the committees were facing an entirely new role.

Perhaps the best example was in the appointment of Roger Blin-Stoyle as chairman of the working party. Blin-Stoyle, chairman of the School Curriculum Development Committee (SCDC), which had only a minor curriculum advisory role, seemed to me to find difficulty in working in an environment where specific recommendations acceptable to a determined government had to be delivered to a tight deadline. It was not long before he was faced by a working group which as soon as the pressure was applied split into a number of factions.

The right was led by Sig Prais, of the National Institute of Economic and Social Research, who made it absolutely clear in the course of the meetings that he had been appointed by Margaret Thatcher. Amongst a number of new experiences this was the first time I had ever served on a committee where a member announced to all and sundry that he had been appointed by the prime minister. Sig Prais did not debate or show any signs, as you need in a working party, of compromising or trying to win people round by argument. He just expressed his views and laid down the way it was to be and became pretty ratty when that did not happen. At this early stage I could best be described as very interested but somewhat detached and remember returning to my office in Humberside expressing relief that I was not the chairman.

The progressives were best represented by two of the education professionals in the group, Hilary Shuard, director of a primary school mathematics group at Homerton College, Cambridge, and Hugh Burkhardt, director of the Shell Centre for Mathematics Education at the University of Nottingham. They both saw the working group as an opportunity to extend the proposals of the January 1982 Cockcroft Committee on Mathematics on which Shuard had served. This committee had been set up by the government in September 1978 – a good indication of the time-scale operated by old-style education working parties – following the recommendations of the education select committee and opened a new era in the teaching of mathematics.

Wilfred Cockcroft, vice-chancellor of the New University of Ulster at Coleraine, and his committee, had broken exciting new ground in the teaching of mathematics, seeking to make it more interesting and less mechanistic so that it was accessible to a broader range of young people. Cockcroft took people into areas such as estimation and the concept of having to be exact in some things but not in others, and the idea that mathematics could be pursued from a practical basis. Children would no longer have to work out how long it would take to fill a bath which never had the plug in, or puzzle over pictures of people mysteriously looking up cliffs to be asked for some obscure reason to calculate the height of the flagpole on the top. From now on children were to be shown that mathematics had a vital and interesting part to play in the solving of real-life problems.

Schools were also asked to ensure that children were taught how to operate calculators and use them in the classrom, a recommendation that was later to be misunderstood and haunt the working party. The overall thrust of Cockcroft, however, was so obviously right that there were dangerous reports that children were actually beginning to enjoy mathematics. The national curriculum working group, perhaps with the exception of Prais, thought that its recommendations should closely follow Cockcroft while combining it with rigour and an ability to master the old skills such as long division. That this was eventually achieved is to the great credit of the group.

Shuard, Burkhardt, and some of the others, however, wanted to go much further. They were against attainment targets and programmes of study, and the thought of testing at the ages of 7 or 11 was anathema to them. As a result they found themselves caught between a commitment which they had obviously given to deliver the report and a rising distaste at the implications of what they came to realise they were being asked to do. Their views were honourably held, but in the circumstances difficult to embrace.

Prais was right in much of his criticism and he was right to insist that children should be given a good understanding of the fundamental processes lying behind mathematics. He was wrong to say that the only way to achieve this was that all children regardless of their ability should do a thousand long divisions every day, as if this had some moral or character building value. All children should also learn all their tables and not be allowed to use calculators until they were 16, he said. Tables yes, but calculators no, even though 5-year-olds can and do go into W.H. Smith and buy them for a few pounds.

The progressives in the group took the view that long division and the learning of tables was no longer necessary because of the invention of the calculator. They also took the damaging view that most children could not do long division or learn their tables, and that since they found these tasks too hard they should not be forced to do them. They seemed to anticipate the day when children would have a calculator grafted into their wrist at birth and they had no time for rote learning of any kind. In one draft report, I wrote that there were some things that, whether they liked it or not, children had to learn until it hurt and that learning could not all be joy. Three of the working group threatened to resign over the phrase 'until it hurt'. The phrase was removed.

In the middle of this heated debate were a number of sensible people looking at both sides of the argument but in the beginning none of the extremists were prepared to compromise as we sat down with a task that nobody understood and the implications of which were enormous. There were seven or eight meetings in the autumn lasting all day, sometimes two, and the first few meetings were very confused.

On one occasion when we met in Stratford upon Avon, Hugh Burkhardt brought his own computer, laid it on the table and as the debates continued typed in his own views, printed them out and passed them round. Every meeting started with the minutes of the last meeting and we spent the first two hours going over them. Any member of the group could submit a paper at any time, so if the argument was going against them, somebody would produce a 20-page paper and hand copies round which the group would then start reading.

The group had to produce an interim report by November after their first six months of deliberation. Nobody could agree anything and the result was, in ministerial terms, an absolute disaster – although some of the working group did point out that in the circumstances it was a miracle that we could tell ministers even vaguely what we were proposing to do. Kenneth Baker, however, was not impressed, letting it be known privately that it was disgraceful, that the working party had failed completely to grasp what was required, that it was part of a conspiracy determined to sink his reforms.

The scene now shifts to the hall of the Law Society in London in November 1988 where I was attending the annual dinner of county council chief executives when pages came to tell me I was wanted on the telephone. I found myself talking to Nick Stuart, a deputy secretary at the Education Department, who told me that Professor Blin-Stoyle felt that he was no longer able to carry on and that his departure would be announced very shortly. He asked me whether I would take the job on and I had never in my life felt less inclined to do anything. Until then I had tried with a singular lack of success to sit in the middle to bring the two sides together, only to earn the opprobrium of Sig Prais simply on the basis that I did not agree with him – a state of affairs that became all too familiar in the era of conviction politics. If you were not entirely in agreement with the regulation point of view you were just as wrongheaded as the most extreme member of the left wing.

Stuart said that Sir David Hancock, the permanent secretary at the department, was at the same dinner and that I should have a word with him. There was I working for a hung council, but which in effect was a Labour administration, being invited to chair a high profile working group which was politically controversial. After much thought I accepted the post on the basis that I would chair the working group on two days a month. I also insisted that civil servants explained the position to the working group. I have often wondered what would have happened had I refused, but it is very hard to say 'no' when the establishment calls on your sense of duty. I must pay due tribute to the council on Humberside for understanding and co-operating.

Never again was a working group report to receive such a hostile response as that given to the mathematics interim report. Writing publicly to Blin-Stoyle, Baker said that he was disappointed, particularly with the failure to outline how the group proposed to deliver age-related targets which could be attempted and assessed at a range of levels to cover pupils of different abilities. The letter added:

> I have to say that I regard it as essential to establish a clear structure of age related targets in order to give teachers, parents and pupils a clear frame of reference against which to measure progress . . . within common targets, accessible to all pupils, it should be possible to specify the normal range of attainment at the key age points . . . I want the group to tackle this as a matter of urgency.

The letter also contained the first official warning about the use of calculators in schools and the battle between modern and traditional teaching methods:

> Your final report will need to recognise the risks as well as the opportunities which calculators in the classroom offer . . . In particular, I want the group to consider the balance between open-ended practical problem solving approaches and the more traditional pencil and paper practice of important skills and techniques.

Prais had decided to write his own note of dissent on the interim report which he sent to Baker. Prais, amongst other things, said that he doubted whether the working group would be able to produce attainment targets and programmes of study as required by the Secretary of State. He said that he did not believe that Cockcroft had adequately considered how much less British pupils knew than foreign children of similar age. He pointed out that multiplication and division of fractions, and areas of circles, for example were taught in Germany and Japan to all pupils and that this could account for their improved economic record. He said that the failure of the working group to understand this began to help him understand why 'so many of you believe that "having fun" is one of the prime objectives of mathematical teaching'. In reply, and quite understandably, Baker said that he would be concerned if the final report did not reflect some of the points Prais made.

More importantly, Baker also made it clear that while being unhappy with the interim report he was not in favour of extreme solutions from either side. He wrote:

> I believe there is scope to find the right balance between the practice and mastery of basic skills and the problem solving approaches

favoured by the Cockcroft report, which have been introduced into our schools only during the last three or four years, with the endorsement of the government.

Perhaps more in hope than conviction, Baker also said that he was not so pessimistic as Prais about the ability of the group to produce attainment targets and programmes of study. Even then, Baker was looking to changes in the future when he added that the original proposals would no doubt be refined in the light of practical experience.

By then the majority of the working group was in any event not well disposed towards the Secretary of State as a result of a meeting with him in September when he told them that the present curriculum was an unmitigated disaster. Most of the members found this too much to accept, particularly with regard to mathematics. He, however, was not prepared to countenance the interim report, which was welcomed by teachers as keeping most of the options open. Baker and the civil servants then began a process of softening up the working group although many of them probably felt they were being roughed up.

Following interim publication, a group of civil servants told the working group that from now on things would have to be done their way. The working party's job was to deliver what was required within carefully prescribed limits. The officials said that ministers feared that we were not going to deliver and were very unhappy with our performance so far.

I became acutely aware that in its implementation and substance this was a Civil Service driven curriculum and not the property of HMI. This was the first evidence of a huge *de facto* power shift in the way education was controlled in England and Wales. The HMI were adjuncts and the inspectors on the working group were extremely helpful, but they were not the driving force: that was the civil servants. The national curriculum was their baby, the first major education reform in Britain that had not been created by the educational professionals.

At that point, and the drama cannot be overstated, the national curriculum hung by a thread. Kenneth Baker made it clear, when I met him for the first time to be appointed chairman of the working group, that we simply had to deliver if the national curriculum was to be saved. The working party had a very tense meeting in London at the beginning of January 1988, the first that I chaired.

I found to my relief that there was a tremendous desire to get on with it. Sig Prais, however, was not there and I never saw him again, learning of his resignation from newspaper reports. He did, however, incur the wrath of Margaret Thatcher who let it be known that she believed he had been wrong to pick up his bat and walk instead of using it to lay about him.

At that first meeting in the new year I told the rest of the group that if anybody wanted to leave, they should go now. This was not a personal invitation to go but if they were thinking of going, now was the time. I asked them all to agree in writing that they would deliver the report, as I felt I could not chair the committee in what was going to be a hectic and difficult six months without that commitment. I stressed with as much conviction as I could find that the working group was not being told what they had to deliver in the report, just to get on and do the work. I also made some points about discipline: for example, that we could not spend two hours every meeting going through the minutes of the last meeting, and that no papers should be submitted except those that had been sent to the secretary beforehand. Apart from Sig Prais, who did not reply to my letter, they all said that they would stay, although Baker had made it plain that even if we lost people from the working group, the report would stand.

The working party well understood that whatever report we came up with was going to be vulnerable to the extreme right wing. The clear task was to compile a report which would as far as possible meet the demands of ministers without sacrificing what the group believed to be the best way of teaching mathematics by sticking to the principles of the Cockcroft report.

During that six months – as if we did not have enough to worry about – there were several publications claiming that practically everybody in the world was better at arithmetic than Britain, although the claims were always dismissed out of hand by the left-wing members of the working group. We were also conscious that the science working group under Jeff Thompson of Bath University was also meeting but we were all far too busy to meet each other. This was most unfortunate. A sharing of knowledge and some jointly formulated definitions of attainment targets and so on would have reduced the incompatibles which surfaced later.

However, officials did not hesitate to tell us that the science working group was proving successful and getting on well. It became clear later that what they were actually doing was annexing half of the geography syllabus! The public position, however, was that as a working group, although not without difficulties, it was more amenable to what the Education Department wanted. In the event the proposals were too complicated and, to the group's general annoyance, had to be considerably reduced.

Meanwhile, the mathematics working group had in effect to undertake a year's work in six months. One of the first and most difficult tasks was to arrive at a reasonable number of attainment targets. At a meeting in a hotel in Hull we pinned all the attainment targets unearthed so far around the walls of the ballroom. There were 354 which were eventually whittled down to 14 and were at the time state of the art. There was a very real achievement in having only 14 attainment targets for maths. The number has now been reduced to five to make it compatible with GCSE but that does not mean that the working group was wrong. The miracle was that we did not have 354!

Although a close run thing, the final report was delivered on time and to everybody's relief was generally well received by both ministers and teachers. The content has never been seriously challenged and nobody has ever suggested what might be cut out. Although his successors went on to make changes, Baker was delighted with the end result and said that to deliver the report on time was a considerable achievement. His pleasure may in part have been sheer relief that the ball game was still on and he might have pushed further for his own line of a greater return to traditional lessons had he thought he could have succeeded. As it was, the report even avoided attack from the right as it quite demonstrably contained standards and rigour. At each stage the group set the standard consciously above existing practice on the basis that if you were going to go anywhere you should go up, a view, incidentally, not shared by the science working group.

The maths report set high standards and contained the things that the right wing wanted while adopting a modern approach, stressing that tables were important, and that while doing thousands of long divisions a day was not necessarily good for the soul when you had a calculator it was important to be able to do a number of them. The report hit the middle ground, appealing to both parents and industry.

On the whole the report was well received by the maths community largely because the mathematics working group had been very careful to emphasise the continuity which it had with Cockcroft. Right through from Cockcroft to the production of the final report the working group embraced the spirit of good teaching which maths teachers supported and had worked for.

The final maths report was workable from the start while that of science was unwieldy. The science working group, having been greatly praised for their interim report when maths was being attacked from all sides, found considerable dificulty in achieving everything they had set out in that first and rather incautious report, which was too detailed and too large. Science was under the same enormous pressure as the mathematics working group to deliver and the group came to regret in the second six months what had been said in the first as it found that room for manoeuvre was seriously curtailed.

Members of the science working group worked closely together without the internal differences facing the mathematics group and in Jeff Thompson they had a very able and affable chairman who got them off to a good start. They quickly realised – which maths had failed to do – that Baker had not set any limits on what they should consider to be appropriate to the science curriculum. In appointing individual subject working groups, members had been given free rein over the subject and when that happens they are never knowingly undersold.

The science working group grasped that this was an opportunity that would never be repeated and must not be missed as an opportunity to make science king of the curriculum. Any misgivings individual members of the group may have had about the national curriculum were overborne by the fact that they passionately believed they could revolutionise science teaching in a world anxious to be taught more. As a result the eventual report was, to say the least, expansionist.

Science had undergone a similar change to that in mathematics where there had been enlightened improvements to traditionally academic subjects. Where it had once been taught by giving a child a science notebook to write down what the teacher said and by the occasional experiment with a bunsen burner, science was now a very practical subject appealing to a wide range of youngsters. Against this background, the working group showed from the very start that no empire was too large by annexing earth sciences from geography, but did it so well that it was hard to attack the proposals.

The final report contained a large number of rather confused attainment targets, but in scientific terms was a very good document which delighted the science community so that any reservations they had about the national curriculum evaporated, if only temporarily. When we started on the consultation exercise we got unanimously supportive remarks which was perhaps not so surprising as the science community had orchestrated the replies.

The maths and science reports were both published on 16 August 1988, two days before NCC came into formal existence. I was still working in Humberside and the only staff I could call on were the people from the SCDC who were full of uncertainties; many of them were openly hostile to the idea of the national curriculum. The virtually non-existent NCC was now to embark on massive and unprecedented consultation exercises for both mathematics and science.

I was straight into the problems which dogged NCC throughout: of never having sufficient time for members to start off and see through processes but simply having to react to the work of officers and pressures from civil servants. If members understood the need for this, they never forgave officers for it.

One of the more incredible minor aspects of the story is that nobody ever knew what consultation really meant. Would NCC be legally up the creek if it did not approach everybody or was it sufficient to make it known that it was seeking information? Policy was being made on the hoof. The only guidance for the legally required consultation was the legislative blueprint which was vague in the extreme over quite fundamental questions such as who, or which organisations, had to be consulted and who should be consulted if possible in addition to anybody who cared to give their views voluntarily. As the law stood there appeared to be two categories: (a) of people and organisations that had to be consulted and (b) of those who could be but need not be. But who and which?

I found myself sitting not in London but in Beverley in Humberside concentrating on the logistics of consulting, on both maths and science, possibly 24,0000 schools, all the organisations which might be involved, political bodies, subject organisations, and unions. The potential list was endless: Longman's *Education Year Book* has around 20 pages listing up to 1,000 potentially interested bodies. The bureaucratic solution as far as the Education Department was concerned was that there was no need to consult either schools or local authorities. The view stemmed from a mixture of the low esteem in which both were held in this new era of education in which the government was going to dictate what was to be taught, and the realisation of the sheer practical difficulties. I passionately believed, however, that the national curriculum would be totally lacking in credibility and that NCC would get off to the worst possible start if it did not consult with schools no matter how enormous the logistical problems.

Everything had to be worked out from scratch to a tight timetable without any of the implications or solutions thought out. The first question which arose was that if NCC was going to ask people what they thought about the various and detailed proposals, how was it to be done? It was quite possible that even if the council did not write to schools, the 24,000 schools would decide to write to the council in addition to the many hundreds of responses that could be expected from individuals. And remember, there were plenty of people around at that time vociferous in their criticism of the national curriculum.

The ill-prepared and ill-staffed council could, therefore, easily find itself in a nightmare situation of having to deal with thousands of uncoordinated responses unless it was possible to construct a questionnaire that was at least partially capable of computer analysis. The situation was incredible: we had not even set up a National Curriculum Council; staff had to be appointed at the same time as the consultation began. How was I, the only member of the staff, going to appoint them?

At its first shadow meeting in York in July, members of the council wished me luck. There was not much else they could do. There was no sub-committee structure which could have provided appointment panels. There was literally nothing. In any event I was still in discussions with the Education Department as to the final staffing structure. Eventually, the initial staffing level was no more than 30. Only half a dozen were ever present before January 1989.

At the point NCC was set up, there had been no planning for what it would require in the long term, whether it would have its own finance department or depend on the DES; would there be interim arrangements? Despite all of this, a minor miracle took place. Two people from the SCDC

– Peter Watkins who became deputy chief executive of NCC, and Jenny Hall, a professional officer with a scientific background – did things beyond any reasonable expectations. Explaining the incredible prospect facing the council I asked Jenny if she would be willing to get maths and science off the ground. All I could offer was the prospect of a job sometime, somewhere in the future although I did not know what it would be, what grade it would be, or even what the structure would be. She was eventually appointed an assistant chief executive of the council.

The three of us began work and enlisted the help of HMI and the National Foundation for Educational Research (NFER) who knew about statistical analyis. Eric Bolton, the senior chief HMI at the time, was extremely generous in seconding HMI with two each for science and maths. The help was invaluable but it was a double-edged sword as the message went down the line to ministers that this new body was so inept that HMI had to do its work, which was far from the truth. A more sensible soul than I would simply have said the whole thing was not on.

With hard work and no little luck the consultations were finished successfully. The breakthrough came after the group working on the consultation devised a questionnaire that was welcomed by the people who received it and in a format that has stood the test of time. There are times in life when you are just astounded at what can be achieved under pressure. For me, the successful conclusion to maths and science was one of those moments. The credit goes to the teams. They literally lived night and day in the bowels of SEAC's offices in Notting Hill Gate.

The other key to the solution was to enlist the help of the much maligned local education authorities as, although the council had to consult the schools, it could not handle 24,000 replies. The council, therefore, took the decision to circulate each school but to ask the local authorities to correlate the answers and return them to the council together with their own response. Apart from the practical benefits, this also helped the council to give the local authorities an important role in the national curriculum right from the beginning. It has to be said, though, that it was a role which some of them did not welcome as many local authorities were not keen to be seen doing anything to assist the introduction of the national curriculum; also the time-scale put them under enormous pressure. The proposals were sent to the schools in the beginning of September to be returned by the end of October and the majority met the deadline.

Before involving the local authorities I spoke to the Society of Education Officers and some senior chief education officers to tell them that it would be the council's policy to involve them as fully as it could. The civil servants warned me that in enlisting the authorities' help, I risked upsetting the Secretary of State. They could only stop the scheme, however, if they came up with a better idea. They did not. They also knew that if this embryonic three men and a dog organisation operating out of one room in

York hired from an office equipment company did not pull the consultation off the whole thing was going to land on the DES. The civil service reluctant approval of the involvement of the local authorities was, therefore, purely pragmatic but I believed it was beneficial both to the authorities and the council in establishing links and in reassuring them that they would have some involvement in the curriculum. It certainly got the council off to a good start.

In spite of all the cynical talk about consultation being a sham, the responses came in huge but controllable numbers with 2,286 for maths and 2,686 for science, including returns from most local education authorities. Those authorities that did not return the questionnaires succeeded only in disenfranchising a sizeable number of schools.

Apart from the handful of replies that said that the whole idea was wrong, that there should be no national curriculum and certainly no National Curriculum Council, the consultation on boths maths and science was surprisingly supportive. The record will also show that in maths and science many of the ideas proposed in the replies were, with two key exceptions, actually adopted.

There were two bones of contention, one in maths and one in science, and they both raised the problem that was to haunt the council continually: the balance between knowledge and understanding, with ministers concentrating on knowledge while the weight of professional opinion lay with understanding.

The problem in mathematics was in profile component 3 (PC3) which grouped together a number of attainment targets concerning the practical application of mathematics. Baker rejected PC3 on the grounds that it would be difficult to test, but more fundamentally because it did not concentrate on a knowledge of mathematical skills. Baker's stance was entirely ideological and gave NCC its first glimpse of the ministerial thrust towards knowledge in the attainment targets which required regurgitation of numbers, dates, and facts. He insisted that the attainment targets should be specific so any suggestion of understanding was considered to be too woolly. Knowledge was all, a position which was to reach its full extension in history under Kenneth Clarke. The argument was lost forever with maths despite the overwhelming support given to the inclusion of the practical profile component by all those who took part in the consultation.

Not for the last time, I found myself in great personal difficulty because although I also wanted PC3, there were sufficient practical problems with it to make it a very difficult thing to enshrine in the statutory orders that would have to follow. Having seen the size of the maths and science reports with all their recommendations, the council was beginning to be concerned about the the total size of the edifice that was being constructed. Oddly enough it was not a fear being shared by ministers. When the penny did drop the hapless NCC would ship the blame.

At the time maths and science were being considered ministers were strongly of the view that they would lay down to the teachers precisely what they would be expected to do and not give them any latitude that might allow them to slide back into the bad old ways.

Ministers were still enthusiastic supporters of a full ten subject compulsory curriculum for all secondary children up to 16. There was panic in the first year at any suggestion that the grand design might be fundamentally flawed. It was to be left to their successors to complain about over-complexity and over-prescription. This was a bit rich as the council had said from early on that the curriculum as originally planned could not work. I and the few professional staff who were there at that time were clearly beginning to see that the whole thing could grow into a monster, but at that stage there was very little we could do.

I told the council that as it would be responsible for the monitoring and evaluation of the national curriculum it would be able to look at the attainment targets and the programmes of study one at a time so that it would be able to recommend changes for improvement in the delivery of the national curriculum. The council accepted that it was better to over-prescribe and then draw back than to under-prescribe and try to tighten up and believed that the best time for change would be in two or three years' time. None of us had any doubts that the master-plan could only work if subjected to drastic pruning.

Following consultation on the working group proposals, it was the duty of NCC to offer its advice to the Secretary of State based on the consultation on the original working group recommendations. The final reports contained two elements: a fair and honest summary of the consultation analysed with the help of the NFER, and NCC's own views.

In the case of the first two reports, the council members had to decide their own views at only their third formal meeting, and most of them knew very little about profile components and attainment targets. In reality, at that stage they had little alternative but to accept the advice of officers – just a handful led by a chairman who was neither mathematician nor scientist. I cling to the belief that it helped to be uncommitted.

The council took the view that the maths PC3 was vital for the whole future of a broad mathematics syllabus embracing the Cockroft report. It believed that it was up to the DES and perhaps SEAC to devise ways of testing it. To stop something on the grounds that it could not be tested was another step towards testing being allowed to control the curriculum rather than the other way round as it should be. This was an early sign that testing could reduce curriculum quality.

The council had neither the expertise nor the knowledge to know how, in the short time available, it could successfully persuade ministers that PC3 could be adapted to meet their concerns. There was massive pressure from the Secretary of State and his civil servants to drop it, and essentially that was what was done.

The council came face to face with the terrible realisation of where it stood in relation to the government. Was it to agree to ministerial wishes or was it going to stand by its own deeply held views based on wide consultation? It was made obvious by officials acting on behalf of ministers that the council would be as good as dead if the Secretary of State rejected its first piece of advice, as seemed likely if it persisted in supporting PC3. The message came through crudely and clearly and the council gave way.

The compromise was to combine the strongest features of PC3 in the two other profile components and to give a public undertaking that the contentious attainment target would be reintroduced after further work. Bearing in mind that the council did not then have a maths specialist this was a respectable enough solution. The proposal was never made again, as it became increasingly clear as we progressed through the other subjects that its chances of success were zero. In any case, as people came to realise the complexity of the whole curriculum they became more and more reluctant to have an extra attainment target of any kind no matter how good it might be.

When I first read the science report in my new guise as chairman of the National Curriculum Council I was very concerned as a non-scientist that it was all things to all men. It was not entirely clear on the attainment targets and programmes of study but nevertheless it was supported by the consultation exercise enthusiastically and totally. There was, however, the inevitable complication and it is that which has stuck in people's minds. This was the twin problem of the argument surrounding dual science, the balanced course which carried two GCSE awards, and the continuation of the traditional three sciences of biology, chemistry and physics, and the amount of time science would occupy in the school week.

A survey into GCSEs that was published while the science group was at work was absolutely damning because it showed that virtually nobody did all three sciences and that girls did biology while boys did physics. If there was a broad and balanced science education it was confined to a very small minority of the population. The picture was gradually changing as the science establishment moved towards the concept of a balanced science course. Unlike the humanities which can be a cover for mixing up and weakening disciplines such as history, geography and economics, balanced science reinforces the three separate elements.

The idea was really opposed only by the traditional science teachers to be found in independent schools but at that point they did not make a great deal of headway. The joy of balanced science is that every child who takes it will have a good working knowledge of all three sciences, but obviously not at the same level as if they had followed all of the three separate courses. The members of the working group had, therefore, a Messianic zeal to sell balanced science and saw the national curriculum as the way to achieve it. In their view the attainment targets could only be delivered by having elements of all three disciplines and they saw national curriculum science as signalling the end of biology, chemistry and physics as separate examination subjects. Here the discord began. Those views were not shared by the traditional boys' independent schools which went on to win the battle to keep the three sciences alongside the balanced course. Their justification was that in their schools the pupils were already, by tackling all three, having a balanced science education. One wonders how many pupils in these schools really do tackle all three of them.

The council thought that the battle had already been won, that the arguments in favour of balanced science were self-evident and that the views of independent schools, which were not compelled to follow the national curriculum, would be peripheral. We were wrong, of course, as they became the most effective lobby in education.

The small National Curriculum Council staff and I had a more immediate problem. To deliver the science curriculum as proposed by the working group was going to take a very considerable amount of the school timetable, between eight and twelve periods out of a 40-period week. Remember, too, that at the time there was no talk of dropping any subjects at key stage 4 as people prepared for the GCSE. There was going to be little room for extra subjects.

The science report was making everybody uncomfortably aware about overcrowding the curriculum, leaving aside complexity. Nobody questioned the expansionist nature of the report in taking over the earth sciences, there was no geography lobby bombarding the council with letters. That was to come later. When the science report was considered in the summer, the embryo NCC, the DES and HMI were all exercised not by the quality of the report but by its size and the implications that it had for teaching time. No matter how the sums were done there was no way we could see that would allow the science report to be accepted in its entirety.

With the unresolved question of the three sciences in the background, Baker, the officials, HMI, and myself came independently to the conclusion that there might have to be two science courses, dual science to take 20 per cent of the curriculum with a new single science course allocated 12.5 per cent of the time. The imperative came from the department but it was accepted that this was a reasonable proposal. The detailed solution, however, was to be found by the council. It became clear, however, that NCC and the government were concerned about two different sets of children.

Council officers were worried about able people who, if they had to follow the full science course, might not be able to follow two languages or the many subjects outside the compulsory curriculum which were none the less important for many students. The council was worried by the fact that by the time there was, say, six periods for mathematics, a minimum eight for science, and another four to six for technology, half the week had gone on scientifically related subjects. While that was arguably what the nation needed, it was a considerable restraint on the rest of the curriculum. Those of us considering the proposals began to think that anything which laid down that half the week was going to be given over to science-based subjects was going to over-restrict those able pupils who wanted to do other things. Our overriding aim was not to tie anybody's hands too much at this stage, and to play for time. The solution was to build in an option, a solution that was seized upon by both ministers and officials.

Given their commitment to rigour and higher standards, ministers could not admit it, but they were concerned about the less able children who would be forced on a diet of science. Not only were they worried about having sufficient science teachers, ministers appeared to be coming to the view that less able children might not be able to cope with all this science and that something more suitable should be found for them.

Despite working to different agendas, we agreed that there was a strong argument for having two science courses at that stage although it need not necessarily be set in stone for ever. The council accepted that with the problem of overcrowding it would be sheer folly to consign every child to a diet which was half 'science'-based and that there ought to be a fall-back position.

Before the proposal was made public, however, we had to work out what a 'single' science course would contain and that is where Jenny Hall's name should be put in lights. Within a space of a few weeks, while also carrying out the consultation, Jenny and the two HMI produced the new course. In order to do so, they worked from six to midnight for two months and during the week slept in camp beds in Notting Hill Gate. One distinguished lady HMI is reputed to have held court for early visitors while still dressed in her night attire. Their solution was to reconsider the full working group report and to produce a course based on the irreducible essentials.

A battle then developed between representatives of NCC and the Education Department because, although they were keen on 12.5 per cent science, they wanted it to be aimed at less able children while the council wanted it to be a tough course so that very able people could or would tackle it. We wanted most people to do dual science but were anxious not to devalue either course. In fact, it would be impossible for most schools to provide both. The council was neverthless keen to keep the single science option available. At the very least it would be a legitimate qualification covering all three individual sciences for able pupils who were not going to specialise in science-based subjects. To put it mildly, the proposal was not popular with the people who replied to the consultation questionnaire, with nine out of ten being against it.

Mark you, nobody had seen the detailed proposals because they were still being worked out, but the concept drove the science community up the wall. Scientists were united against NCC with the divisions over the teaching of the three separate sciences to follow later. Whatever happened, scientists did not want to see the introduction of what they believed would be a watered-down science course. NCC's solution was far from that. None the less scientists liked the working party report so much that they wanted that and nothing else.

The opposition mounted as non-scientists were joined by others who suspected that yet again less able children were going to be discriminated against by being offered sub-standard science. The controversy reached its peak as the council met to consider its recommendations on both maths and science. Remember that NCC only came into being in a real sense in January 1989. Crucial decisions, however, had to be made in the autumn of 1988. At that moment, the members knew little about the role of NCC, having a staff of four and still no headquarters.

The council had before it the two science courses together with the results of the consultation, but because of the quite inescapable time constraints they had only seen the details a day or two before they had to make their decision. There was no way that members of the council could have shared in the work that had gone into the two reports. There they were in the full glare of publicity with the whole weight of the science establishment against the proposals that they were being asked to agree. Baker, while not aware that the single award science was a a very tough course, had made it publicly clear that he was in favour of two sciences. Critics of the council refused to believe that the proposal had come from NCC.

At the crucial counsil meeting there was little debate on the maths report apart from considerable regret at the loss of profile component 3. Assurances that it would resurface were accepted. When the meeting reached science the council had one of the best debates that I have ever attended on the value of education, on the future of the national curriculum, and on the importance of science. At the end of that debate the council decided unanimously and for the best of reasons that there had to be two sciences. They could not prejudice future flexibility in the national curriculum. Many of the members had been concerned that single science might be an easy option for schools to use for the less able, particularly if they were short of science teachers, but were reassured when they saw that it was anything but. The world then descended on the fledgling National Curriculum Council. Here at last was proof positive that the council was entirely in the hands of the Secretary of State. He had told it what was required and it had submitted like the poodle it was. We were in truth minded to be Yorkshire terriers.

NCC made statement after statement that its decision was a free one in the wider interests of the curriculum as a whole. It was largely laughed at, and certainly not believed. The decision was not made with gladsome minds but, ironically, bearing in mind all the other occasions in the future when the council was put under ministerial pressure, the decision on science was genuinely free. On this occasion the council's views happened to accord with the views of the Secretary of State. The experience over science was beginning to make it uncomfortably clear that the council could not win. Was it there to take the blame?

The council, well aware that it was working in a vacuum, wrote to Baker to say:

> Council wishes to draw to the Secretary of State's attention that it has yet to develop its view on the framework of the curriculum and has put forward its recommendations for a single award science course in the absence of this framework.

The letter went on to say that Baker should do all he could to encourage schools to develop courses leading to the dual award and offer it to the majority of pupils. It was subsequently agreed that whatever else they did, schools had to offer the dual course.

In both maths and science, the real work of NCC was in suggesting detailed improvements to make the statutory proposals more user-friendly and less complicated. The council's final recommendations on mathematics and science to the Secretary of State were better than they would have been without consultation. At the time nobody thought that and the cynicism remained, but the fact was that the consultation was largely listened to and embraced within the final reports. The national curriculum had been rescued from the brink.

The debate then soon moved into SEAC territory when it began its review of the number of GCEs to be approved. When it came to science, SEAC, after a great deal of discussion, took the view in March 1990 that GCSEs should be offered only for the two national curriculum science courses, and that examinations in the three separate sciences should be discontinued in the interests of providing a broad education. Until then, nearly everybody had believed that the curriculum changes would primarily affect state schools, but once GCSEs were involved the independent schools became vitally concerned. In any event, the science community was saying that the integrity of the three sciences was secured within dual science and that students would be perfectly able to move on to A-levels. Independent schools, however, took a different view and became very vociferous. A battle royal began. The views of NCC were sought and were that it was not possible to deliver national curriculum science through the individual sciences unless all three were studied. That was, and remains, a very tall order for all but the most able pupils.

The pressure then came to alter the national curriculum in such a way that it would be possible to get round it without following either dual science or all three separate sciences. There was only one answer. If there was to be a national curriculum, examinations had to cover the whole of the national curriculum not just part of it. NCC decided that dual science was sufficient and that it was unneccesary to have the three sciences. It did not have a view as to whether examinations in the three should continue, that was up to others to decide. NCC was, however, adamant that the national curriculum could best be delivered by dual science and only reluctantly agreed that it could be replaced if all three separate sciences were followed.

It was during this epic battle that the incredible power of the independent schools became evident. John MacGregor had taken over from Baker in the summer of 1989 and it fell to him to resolve the science argument. His readiness to listen to the independent schools was one of the few things about MacGregor which really shook and disappointed many in state education. He had many meetings with them and he was the one who really started cracking the whip over SEAC. He may have been right in the end but he can be criticised for listening too much and too overtly to the independent lobby on that and on other matters.

At one of my regular meetings with him at the height of the argument and while he was still making his mind up, he sought my views and I told him the council's position. He made his equally clear: a Conservative government could not prevent people from doing things that were not outside the law unless there were compelling reasons, and as far as he was concerned, there were not in this case. He said that there was no mileage in it for him not to allow the three sciences and that if the arguments in favour of dual science were as strong as he was being told then market forces would determine that dual science would prevail. Put that way it was hard to disagree with him when he announced in July 1990 that he would allow schools to continue to teach all three sciences.

I am bound to say that I began to think that the scientists were wasting their time in trying to win battles that did not need to be won. Providing all three sciences were taught it did not much matter how. What has happened now is that independent schools are either making their pupils do all three sciences, and for the most able people there is no harm in that, or they are going for the dual science. The success of the national curriculum, and the ultimate gain for education, is that there are no longer children in this country not studying all three sciences however they are being taught.

4

A QUESTION OF GRAMMAR

English had as shaky a start into the national curriculum as mathematics with the working group running into the same polarisation of views about traditional lessons. In maths, the argument was about calculators and long division. In English, the debate centred on the teaching of grammar, the books that children should read, and the importance of reading, writing and spelling.

The members of the English working group found that they were in more general agreement than the members of the mathematics group, but that was eventually to lead them into considerable disagreement with Kenneth Baker. The group took as its starting point the report of the committee chaired by Sir John Kingman, vice chancellor of Bristol University.

The Kingman report was something of an embarrassment to the government as it covered much of the same ground as the English working group had to consider. Kingman was still sitting when the national curriculum was introduced, which is why Baker was unable to set up the English working group at the same time as the mathematics and science groups as he had intended. The three subjects were the first national curriculum lessons planned for primary schools in September 1989.

When it was finally published, the Kingman report was a disappointment. Whereas Cockroft had pulled it off in maths, satisfying nearly everybody and with no great argument about standards, the Kingman committee became bogged down in a fundamental problem. Many of those involved in the teaching of English had moved very considerably to the left in all the touchstone areas of literature, grammar, reading, writing and spelling. The prevailing view appeared to be that English teaching did not necessarily have to include Shakespeare and Dickens, and should concentrate on twentieth-century works. Whether this is right or wrong is a matter of personal taste. My own view is that a nation's children, whatever their ability, should have some contact with the classics in the nation's literary history. Shakespeare would clearly be included in that, and it would be hard to have a GCSE without some reference to him.

A more fundamental problem was a growing feeling that teachers should no longer correct mistakes in spelling or punctuation, such as the use of full stops and capital letters, because it obstructed children in their creative writing. Formal grammar teaching had largely disappeared as part of the philosophy that had been seen in mathematics: children could only learn through enjoyment and should not be inhibited by the use of such words as noun, pronoun and verb. They would learn the structure of language through use. The same arguments dictated that children should never be asked to learn a list of spellings because it was mechanistic, with the words being used out of context. Children should learn spelling by putting their own thoughts on paper and then being gently reminded when a word was misspelt in context. Too many teachers did not even do that.

The swing to extreme teaching methods started from the quite genuine belief that children would be put off any kind of writing if every time they started something imaginative they were stopped short by a teacher to correct spelling or punctuation. The new teaching methods also became a very convenient excuse for dropping standards in marking and correction. The teaching of English moved far away from traditional values and standards. In its place came the drive for imagination and creative thinking and writing.

That has much to commend it. I cannot have been the only person of my generation to leave school without realising that people still wrote poetry. Schools did tend to inhibit imagination. Creative writing in schools has reached a quality it would never have achieved in the 1960s and there is much publishable material that comes from quite young children. Children are very much better at expressing themselves and probably have a deeper appreciation of literature which comes from their own attempts at making it. Once again, a good idea went wrong because some schools lost their sense of proportion and the changes went much too far. A sense of balance would have made it possible to combine an under standing of the structure of language and its correct use, which includes spelling and legibility, while continuing to nurture imaginative and excit- ing work. The government expected Kingman to redress the balance. It did not.

The Kingman committee was asked to recommend a model of the English language, whether spoken or written, which would serve as the basis of how teachers are trained to understand how the English language works and which would also inform professional discussion of all aspects of English teaching; recommend the principles which should guide teachers on how far and in what ways the model should be explicit to pupils, to make them conscious of how language is used in a range of contexts; and to recommend what, in general terms, pupils need to know about how the English language works and in consequence what they should have been taught, and be expected to understand on the working of the language, at 7, 11, 14 and 16.

Kingman was by no means an extremist report but it is fair to say that while it made some concessions to the need to raise standards it rejected a return to formal grammar teaching, making it clear that the only way to teach children English, including grammar and spelling, was by stimulating their interest and correcting mistakes as they went along. The structured form of teaching, where children learned one thing in one lesson and another in the next, had gone.

One of the committee's few concessions was to insist that every child should be able to write and speak standard English. The Kingman report was seen as being the work of educational professionals. Baker did nothing to promote its recommendations and deflected interest by setting up the English working group on 29 April 1988, the day he published Kingman, in the hope that the working party would share his views.

The working group chairman was Brian Cox of Manchester University, who had served on the Kingman committee. He had also been a member of the pressure group which had produced the right-wing Black Papers on Education in the 1980s and it was widely believed that Baker had chosen him in order to bring English teaching back to the more traditional approach. The unspoken brief was to undo Kingman.

Clues to the government's intentions could be found in the brief to the working group which asked it to design a teaching programme which would ensure that all school-leavers would be competent in the use of written and spoken English, whether or not it was their first language. The group was also asked to ensure that their recommendations on learning about language and its use should draw upon the English literary heritage; should promote the reading of great literature and the knowledge and appreciation of literature; and should indicate the types of literature which all pupils should cover in the course of their studies.

The English working group was set up in the normal way with civil servants and HMI making their recommendations, but because Cox was in the chair it was seen to be rather right wing. The membership of the ten-strong group, however, was in the main taken from the professionals in English teaching and, like the people in the mathematics and science groups, they were unaware of the pressures they were going to face. The only attempt to bring any obvious excitement to the working group was the selection of the writer Roald Dahl who resigned within a matter of months after falling out of sympathy with the aims of his colleagues.

The delay in setting up the working group meant that it was unable to publish an interim report and produced the primary school proposals before tackling secondary school English. This did present difficulties but it was the only way to meet the now all too familiar tight deadline – in this case September 1988. The secondary report was due at the end of May 1989.

To everybody's surprise the primary report was on the soft side and was more identifiable with Kingman than the wishes of the Secretary of State. Cox, it seemed, had been misrepresented and was anxious to dissociate himself from the right wing. He had also charmed the civil servants attached to the committee into delivering something that was not entirely within the script.

As a result the working group reported: 'We find ourselves in agreement with the underlying assumptions of the Kingman report and in essentials with its conclusions.' When the long and diffuse primary report was published it drew immediate criticism from Baker and Mrs Thatcher. Baker labelled it as being too woolly, particularly in regard to grammar and any systematic teaching of reading. He could hardly be blamed: the working group had simply failed to grasp that nothing less than a firm comittment to grammar, however it was described, would be acceptable to the government. Instead they echoed Kingman:

> Grammar is only one part of a study of language . . . terms are necesssary but should be taught in and assessed in context for a purpose . . . likely to arise because of problems which pupils have discovered for themselves . . . pupils should not do labelling exercises . . . it is not sensible to propose a definitive list of terms.

Officials let it be known to education correspondents in a non-attributable briefing that the Secretary of State believed too little attention had been paid to the teaching of grammar. The report, said the unidentified officals, was not clear about what children should know at different stages of their schooling. Neither was Mr Baker convinced that the teaching methods suggested would adequately equip children for the assessment tests at 7 and 11.

Publicly, he told the council to consider redefining the attainment targets so that they were sufficiently precise, and to propose ways in which teaching methods could ensure that grammatical structure and terminology were appropriately reflected. When it came to reading and writing, Baker said the proposals were a useful start for further work but that those for reading needed to be more comprehensive, while writing should be strengthened to give greater emphasis to the place of grammatical structure. English in the national curriculum was not getting off to a good start.

There was some common ground when the working group and Baker did agree that while all children should be taught standard English there should be no right or wrong approach to the language. In some circumstances, for example where friends were talking to each other, it would be perfectly acceptable for children to use phrases such as 'we was'; 'he ain't done it'; 'she come here yesterday'; 'they never saw anybody'; 'he writes really quick'; 'theirselves'. The working group agreed, however, that standard English, both written and spoken, must be taught to all as it served particular functions – for example, in the education system and professional life, in public and formal uses, in appplying for and keeping jobs, and particularly in print. A grand debate followed in which standard English became confused with 'proper' English, perhaps best defined as Lord Reithian BBC diction which led to fears that there would be a campaign against dialects. Had that indeed been the case, many of us would have been in considerable difficulty.

The report also included an ill-advised primary booklist which consigned Enid Blyton to a shelf under the library counter. I rather regretted her complete exclusion and wondered why children would be allowed to read *Just William*, but not *The Famous Five*. Charles Dickens, the Revd W. Awdry with *Thomas the Tank Engine*, Frank Muir and James Herriot, Oscar Wilde and Beatrix Potter, were all included among the 200 recommended authors. The report added that few children would actually want to read Wilde, Dickens and Rudyard Kipling on their own but they might prove suitable for teachers to read to children. Other authors listed were Hans Christian Andersen; Terry Jones, the Monty Python performer; Penelope Lively, a Booker Prize winner; Ted Hughes, the Poet Laureate; Jules Verne, Spike Milligan; Roger McGough, the poet; and Dr Suess.

In selecting books the report said:

> The language used should be accessible to children but should also make demands, and extend their language capabilities. The story should be capable of interpretation at different levels so that children can return to the book time and time again with renewed enjoyment in finding something new. Most important, the books selected must be those children enjoy.

The books on the list did meet the criteria but no doubt so did many of those other authors who are popular with children and teachers. Any attempt to make the list exemplary would simply stir up prejudices.

Baker was initially attracted to the idea of a booklist but backed off when he saw the difficulties. The list provoked a hostile reaction from teachers, parents and publishers alike, and was dropped from subsequent reports largely on the grounds that any list, no matter how advisory, tended to become the required standard rather than the guidance it was intended to be. The council also did not believe that the list was sufficiently comprehensive and told the working group that it was a non-starter. Baker quite rightly wanted more examples of the types of literature that might be used and was given them but there were no more booklists. The primary booklist turned out to be difficult enough and the working group knew they would be in real trouble if they attempted to provide one for secondary children.

Problems intensified when it came to the council's statutory consultation on the primary report which had to be conducted while the working group was still considering its secondary proposals. Writing to Baker, the group made a brave attempt to secure the future: 'We shall be assuming that the principles outlined in our first report are accepted, and that we should build on our recommendation there to provide continuity and progressions. We need to know soon if this assumption is ill-founded.' The working group was told sooner than it expected as ministers lost no time in making it clear that the report was unacceptable in its original form, not least because it was causing considerable disquiet in Downing Street.

My own view was that a national curriculum English course needed more teeth than the one being offered by the working group. Rigour and improved standards would only come if the clock was turned back a little bit. I faced an immediate problem when a handful of NCC staff threatened to resign after being told that the council would have to rewrite at least some parts of the Cox report and in particular to insist that some grammar – even if it was called a knowledge of language – was taught in primary schools. The council was, however, determined that the report had to be toughened. Whether it was tough enough in the end is a matter of opinion.

Cox and the English working group, which was still in session, were extremely upset by what the National Curriculum Council had done to their report. They said in clear terms that the council was prejudicing what they would be able to say in the secondary proposals; that they were no longer free agents. They should be allowed to report to the Secretary of State what they determined to be in the best interests of the country's children. I would have said the same in their shoes but the council had to deal with the practicality of the situation. Because I was not allowed to meet the working group and have a free dialogue with them I was not able to explain the position. It may even have been possible to have come to terms with them. Every piece of common sense said that once the National Curriculum Council had been set up there should be clear links with the subject working groups.

The Education Department, however, predictably fell back on the argument that if the council was to be responsible for consultation it could not be party to the original proposals. Clearly the council should not be allowed to influence final conclusions but it was self-evident that as it knew how attainment targets and programmes of study worked, professional and technical advice at an early stage could have prevented subsequent difficulties. The council could also point out any cross-curricular themes that were emerging as other subjects were developed.

The fact that the working group still had to complete its remit created a difficult situation which was made very much worse by the quite fundamental division between them and some NCC officials on one side and Baker and myself on the other. This led to a stormy passage during the consultation stage in which the people who responded to the council questionnaire were in broad agreement with the working group proposals. By the time the consultation had been completed there were few problems with NCC staff or NCC itself and I began to believe that there would now be a period of calm. This was not to be.

Shortly before the revised report was due to be sent to members for them to read prior to the council meeting which was to approve it for delivery to the Secretary of State, I received a telephone call from a very agitated official who said the report was totally unacceptable; the day before she had said the exact opposite. She said that the council meeting should be cancelled and the report rewritten, and that this was an instruction from the Secretary of State. Remaining extraordinarily calm under the circumstances, I asked her to tell me the four or five most unacceptable passages and I would try to accommodate them if she called me back within the hour. The hour went by with no response so I telephoned her to discover that there were no fundamental points she could raise. My response was to thank her for telling me the situation as she saw it but that whatever happened the council would have to make its own decision. There was no more talk about the Secretary of State but when I asked why the original call had been made the civil servant concerned told me that the working group had threatened to resign if they did not get their way. There was never an acceptable explanation for this extraordinary incident but it appeared that the official, who had become close to the working group, had reacted before taking further advice.

The council heard no more about it and members of the working group did not resign, if only, one presumes, because they were concerned as to who would take their places. One is forced to the conclusion that in this case officials believed that NCC could be manipulated while the working group could not, and clearly a mass resignation would have been very damaging as it still had to complete work on the secondary proposals. Mystifyingly, the civil servants involved with the English working group believed the report would be acceptable – even though ministers had made it perfectly clear that it would not – and did not want the council to tamper with it.

As a result of all this and despite the pressures, including those from Downing Street to toughen up the final report, the working group managed to prevent the real and deep changes that I had expected. To my surprise, the final report was very largely accepted by Baker who was relieved that NCC had retrieved a fair amount.

The primary English curriculum that was presented to Parliament in March 1989 laid down that children should be taught grammatical terms such as sentence, verb, tense, noun, and pronoun, and use standard English throughout the curriculum. Children would also be encouraged to memorise the spelling of words and to compile a list of words they had used, but it was still largely up to teachers as to how they approached the use of grammar and the teaching of standard English which had to be used in written work. The national curriculum was therefore given an English blueprint that was softer and less rigorous than that of either mathematics or science, but I made a mental note to return to English at some later date to redress the balance further.

The only major change to NCC's proposals was the requirement by Baker, a poetry lover, that primary school children would have to learn poetry by heart. This was the first and most harmless example of direct ministerial interference in what should be taught in the national curriculum, quite unlike what was to follow in history under Kenneth Clarke. Harmless as it was, Baker's intervention was the first indication that ministerial whim could be enshrined in law.

Following Baker's approval of the final primary report, which gained general approval, word came in a roundabout fashion that Downing Street was still not pleased. In an attempt to keep at least some options open, Baker agreed only to implement key stage 1 leaving the rest to be dealt with in the second English report in June 1989.

Having initially been kept away from Cox I saw him on two or three occasions before the working group published its secondary proposals, and he asked for my views on some of the later drafts. We found that there was a great deal of common ground. My feeling is that Cox, having been forced to go out of his way to say that he was not the property of the right wing, was quite happy to be brought back into the middle again.

When the working group moved on to the consideration of the secondary report it had to decide on how to handle language and literature in the English curriculum. The group endorsed the council's view that English is indivisibly both its language and its literature. The report recommended that there should be a single national curriculum English covering both language and literature and, by implication, one GCSE, and that all the attainment targets would apply to both components.

The debate over whether language and literature should be separated is still rattling on. It is a moot point whether language and literature are best provided by being separate or by being unified. I tend to the view that they are so intimately related that they should be together, but that no fundamental principles are involved. It may have something to do with the number of periods English would claim on the timetable. The view of the council was quite clear. If children were to be given a proper education in English they would have to learn language, and that means grammar, and they would also need a significant acquaintance with literature.

Within that, some attention must be paid to the heritage of English literature but it is equally important that children have access to modern work. There must be no question of cutting them off from that. I also took the view that if people were determined to make a particular study of English literature there was no harm in having an extra examination in the same way as children were allowed to study an extra language, for example.

The secondary report was initially sent to Baker but John MacGregor had taken over by the time the final decisions were made and little of real consequence was changed. Those people who took part in the consultation were in broad agreement with the proposals. There was some concern about the place of drama in the curriculum but only 3.2 per cent wanted it to have its own attainment target. A majority regretted what they described as an over-emphasis on the functional use of language at the expense of the personal and the imaginative. The working group also engendered strong disapproval by excluding rigour and commitment from the attainment targets. One-third accepted the proposals that grammar should be taught by being introduced systematically in discussion when needed while another third were in favour of more formal grammar teaching. The council did achieve some modifications to the place of grammar in the curriculum, but it now seems that the debate is to begin all over again.

Had I been given my own way on English, I would have gone considerably further and been more specific. Had the council published clear guidance on the teaching of reading for example, I am convinced that the controversy over falling standards and the national curriculum could have been avoided. Clear guidance would also have avoided a great deal of the discussions about the place of English language and literature. As it was, the opportunity was lost and it will be quite difficult to regain the ground. The irrelevant recent reductions in GCSE course-work and changes in the literature paper have not left teachers of English in the best frame of mind for rational and reasonable discussion.

5

A REAL REVOLUTION?

The one truly revolutionary subject to enter the national curriculum has been technology. Indeed it would not be an exaggeration to say that it was invented for the curriculum and has gone on to become part of the extended core, together with English, mathematics, science and a modern language, which will remain fully compulsory subjects until 16.

Because it is compulsory for all, from the very brightest child to the less able, technology can become the vehicle for breaking down the academic and vocational divide which has bedevilled British education for so long. For that reason alone technology has been popular with politicians of all shades. The only constructive discussion I had at the first meeting with Tim Eggar shortly after he had been appointed Minister of State in August 1990 was on the need to improve vocational education in schools. He had a very good vision of 14 to 19 education and understood that if education at 14 could mix academic and vocational skills it would help children to make sensible choices at 16. Technology can be the beginning of that revolution as for the first time the thinkers will be forced to make and the makers will be forced to think.

From the moment the Education Reform Bill was published, technology appeared as one of the foundation subjects although there is an air of mystery about how it came to be there. Technology was quite the most revolutionary thing in what otherwise was a traditional ten-subject curriculum and at first sight seemed to sit uneasily alongside the other nine.

The parentage of technology has never been made clear although it is likely that Baker had a hand in it, having been the man who introduced computers into schools when he was a junior trade minister. He certainly went on to become an enthusiastic supporter of the new subject which was not the initial position of many of Her Majesty's inspectors of schools. Individual subject inspectors were concerned to preserve the old divisions of craft, design and technology, home economics, art and design, business studies, and information techology that were to be consumed by the newcomer. Even now there are pockets of resistance amongst some inspectors, schools and teachers, and there has always been confusion between technology and information technology.

The most likely source of technology as a national curriculum subjects is from an amalgam of civil servants and Baker who together felt it was time to do something to remove the grip of woodwork and metalwork for boys and needlework and domestic science for girls, following the successful experience of the Technical and Vocational Education Initiative (TVEI). The solution was to be found in technology, which neatly fell into Conservative philosophy as it had clear links with industry and could be used to develop entrepreneurial skills in the youngest of children. This should be borne in mind when the reasons for a hasty review are sought.

Whoever wishes to claim the credit must also concede that they lost sight of the fact that design had become an integral and successful part of art. Strangely, the architects of the curriculum left art out of technology even though it is an intrinsic part of both subjects. The decision to allow art to stand on its own was to cause some difficulties when the art working group was set up.

When technology first appeared on the agenda of the National Curriculum Council it is fair to say that nobody was clear what it was and it was left to the working group to invent it. The group began work under Lady Parkes, a governor of the BBC with a particular interest in education. The wife of Edward Parkes, vice-chancellor of Leeds University, she proved to be a very determined and successful chairwoman. She had close links with both education – although she proudly proclaimed that she was not an educationist – and industry.

Members of the group began their deliberations without even knowing the title of the course they were considering. The Act had designated the subject as technology but the working party had been set up as the design and technology group. They knew only what it was not going to be: it was not to be craft, design and technology (CDT) or any of its individual parts, each of which were no longer considered to be desirable on their own. The only guidance given to the council was that it was an entirely new subject and was capable of radically changing the way things were taught in schools. The stark reality was that while the mathematics, science, and English working groups in their early meetings might have been totally baffled about attainment targets and programmes of study, their members were in no doubt what the subjects were. Technology was a clean sheet. Baker watched and nurtured technology through the many occasions when it appeared that the obvious difficulties might just have overwhelmed the working group. There was never a day when it would not have been easier to give up than go on.

The definition that finally came to be given was that technology demanded that children had to first identify a problem or a need, design a solution, make whatever was required, and then evaluate the outcome in aesthetic, commercial and environmental terms. Here at last was a school lesson concerned with generating ideas, making and doing. Industrialists could hardly contain their approval as they saw this as the basis for all commercial enterprises.

There are a number of reasons for the controversy surrounding technology. One is undoubtedly the reaction of the supporters of the traditional craft subjects. It was, and is, difficult to get the balance right between craftsmanship for its own sake – the mortise and tenon joint brigade on the one hand and the *Blue Peter* milk top and glue team on the other. The reality is that too much time had been spent in too many schools on high standards which had no practical relevance in the world of work. But when a new subject is seen as a threat the standards argument can be potently deployed.

The introduction of technology also led to facing up to the fact that there would have to be a certain abandonment of standards and rigour which were the driving forces of all the other subjects. When it came to making things, for example, it was realised that the craftsmanship would not always be of the highest quality, which is inevitable if technology is to be followed by all children.

The working group was determined from the outset that technology would be for all, but knew that in the past the component subjects had not been chosen by able children and that was going to have to change. They were aware that there was going to be no room in the national curriculum for the old subjects on their own and also knew that room would have to be found for information technology. They did not know then whether it would be considered as a whole subject with a comparable number of periods to the traditional subjects or whether there would be a GCSE at the end of it and were, therefore, in a quandary as to how to proceed. They were bewildered, but there was a feeling of excitement that if a definition could be found then a whole new world awaited. At the same time a number of people at NCC realised that technology was a Trojan horse which could throw the curriculum wide open and challenge traditional subject barriers. Lady Parkes and some of the working group arrived independently at broadly the same conclusion.

The Chinese walls between NCC and the working group remained but there was no determined attempt to keep us apart. Having finally managed to speak to Cox about English I was determined to talk to Lady Parkes before anything was finally submitted as the council and the working groups should be helping each other. She accepted at face value the promise that NCC would not attempt to influence the outcome of the working group but might be able to help along the way. When we did meet there was a common feeling that the definition that was finally agreed did transcend subject boundaries and should be capable of delivery through almost any subject.

The weight of opinion then was that it would not be necessary to do any of the old craft subjects at all and that technology could be delivered in history or geography, mathematics or science. The council saw it as an activity which drew on knowledge and skills from every subject. In primary schools technology could be handled by teachers who were originally terrified of the very word until it was explained to them what the subject was and they realised how exciting it could be. The attraction of technology as it ultimately emerged is its simplicity.

The idea may now have been subverted but the original pure and simple concept was that technology could and should permeate all subjects and that it may not have needed any of its own space in the timetable. Indeed, there was even the view that it might be a mistake to treat it separately as its real effect would be felt if every subject had to take it on board. At this point its place in key stage 4 was unclear, as was the form it might take at GCSE.

With the publication of the working group report there was little short of uproar from the old guard. Home economics teachers could see there was little room for them in the national curriculum unless they changed. Teachers of CDT and information technology felt that they had been cheated because until the report was published they had both believed that they were all of technology rather than just a part of it.

The final definition had still to be resolved and all the teachers who believed they were an integral part of technology became very agitated and the situation became quite fraught. The working group performed a miracle in taking this amorphous concept that nobody knew how to deal with and producing a solution that found general approval. As people try to rewrite history and apportion blame, it is worth remembering this.

In dealing with technology the council found that it had rather a different role than with mathematics, science and English in that it joined with the working group in fighting for the acceptance of the subject rather than having too many worries about what their proposals might be. Successful efforts were made to reduce the jargon, but 'artefacts' stubbornly persisted.

Following the statutory consultation the council made what it saw as a significant advance with an excellent report which broke new ground and offered all pupils the prospect of a broad coherent education in what has arguably been one of the weakest areas in the English education system: a relevant and demanding approach to what happens in the real world. Leaving the vested interests to one side, the working group report was welcomed equally by schools, industry and NCC, all of which agreed that technology was something that could be taught across the traditional subjects.

The council's recommendations following the consultation were clearer and the confusion over the name of the subject was to be resolved once and for all: it was to be technology. Consultation had shown that the majority of people involved in delivering the curriculum agreed that none of the subjects which made up technology could on their own cover the proposed syllabus. Together the council and the working group had demolished the most persistent criticism of the national curriculum as a strait-jacket and provided the opportunity to re-examine and rethink how everything was taught in schools. They were only too aware that with all its early uncertainties it might be a easy target for subject traditionalists.

The council's proposals sent in November 1989 to John MacGregor, the new Secretary of State, challenged schools, particularly secondary schools where technology would have to be taught by departments in co-operation and annexed by none, to create a new approach to teaching. Technology was MacGregor's first foray into the dangerous waters of the national curriculum, and uncharacteristically the National Curriculum Council used some strong language to underline the importance it attached to the new subject, telling him that if technology failed the country would fail to prosper. It said that the retraining of teachers would have to begin imm-ediately and for the first time in presenting its reports, NCC pointed out the resource implications of the proposals saying that more money would have to be found if technology was to successfully enter primary schools the following September. It was never forthcoming.

The council warned MacGregor: 'The current lack of expertise and confidence among teachers, particularly primary teachers is a cause for concern . . . Initial teacher training courses will need modification, with a particular challenge being the training of non-specialist primary teachers.' Technology, it said, would prepare children to meet the needs of the twenty-first century and cope with a rapidly changing society.

> Business and industry need young people who have the vision to combine enterprise, initiative and imagination with the knowledge and skills to solve problems and create the nation's wealth. If this need cannot be met then our national development will not prosper, a failing that will have dire consequences for the future.

As the council worked on its final recommendations to MacGregor there was tension between Lady Parkes and some of its members as she wanted to go further in breaking down the subject barriers and in providing resources than the council thought was achievable. In practical terms, bearing in mind time and resource, delivery would have to involve exist-ing subjects such as craft, design and technology, home economics, and business studies.

Lady Parkes would have no truck with individual lobbies such as home economics or CDT who simply wanted the national curriculum to include their subjects in their own right. There was a point when the science lobby also wanted to take over technology, arguing that it was very largely based on experiments, an argument that neither NCC nor Lady Parkes accepted. Technology could and should be taught within science but it could not be exclusive to science.

The final report which settled on the two profile components of design and technology and information technology was well received, with a general acceptance that schools needed the new subject. Welcoming the report, MacGregor, who as a junior minister had once been in charge of small businesses, said:

> If we are to meet the needs of the economy and of individuals over the coming decades we must apply scientific and other knowledge in imaginative ways. We will need to pay particular attention to all aspects of design, including cost, quality and appearance.

Once technology was up and running there was tremendous pressure on the council staff as apparently every school in the country wanted help and support in setting up technology courses. The council was having difficulty in financing and recruiting staff, and technology ended up with only two professional officers for 24,000 schools.

When the concept had been accepted there were immediate attempts to take it over, with some schools wanting to build technology laboratories amidst general disagreement about whether they should be the same as CDT or home economics rooms or something quite different. There was a strong feeling that if you did have such labs there was a danger of frightening off primary schools who were beginning to see technology in a new light.

Teachers in the old craft subjects fought desperately to hang on to their position by arguing that technology was really only CDT writ large, a view that has meant that in the country as a whole there is no consistency. In retrospect it might have been better if the council had been more specific about how schools might organise provision for lessons, either by appointing a head of technology or a co-ordinator to plan lessons in conjunction with other teachers.

Technology as envisaged by the working group, with sophisticated applications such as control technology, is alive and well in many schools – not least in the independent sector where it has become academically acceptable with more and more pupils following it at A-level instead of science or engineering. Significantly, independent schools tend to be better equipped than state schools and many have new technology wings donated by parents or industry. To be taught properly technology does require a great deal of equipment and a wide range of materials. State schools are probably well equipped with lathes and cookers but these are no longer central to requirements, except, say, for those pupils taking specific GCSEs in home economics, or CDT.

Many heads of independent schools claim that just as important as the resources available to them is their ability to act swiftly in terms of curriculum innovation. There is some truth in that and it is easy to see why they so impressed MacGregor. There is also much superb technology going on in state schools. The most exciting things I have seen in recent visits to schools have been in technology; so have some of the most depressing. In too many, technology is being used as little more than another name for the old subjects brought together and the situation is now confused. Some schools have had to be continually reminded by the National Curriculum Council and SEAC that the demands of the curriculum cannot be satisfied by teaching only one of the component parts. On the whole, though, technology has tended to disturb the traditional subject boundaries and is less gender-biased than the subjects it replaced.

The introduction of technology as a single subject within the national curriculum has also improved the quality of teaching, as how ever much it is distorted schools do have to provide documentary evidence that they are meeting the original definition of identifying a need and then meeting it. Pupils' project books are worth looking at wherever the subject is well taught – they are clear, logical, and imaginative. Some of the resultant designs are well worth patenting. Simply making a cake, however, because a need for it had been identified would not qualify. Technology has forced girls' schools to rethink their strategy and I believe that many girls were not best served by home economics and needlework alone – which is not to say that pupils should not be taught to be self-sufficient, nor that home economics has been less than excellent and relevant both for girls and boys.

Technology leavened a subject-orientated curriculum and is most closely related to vocational qualifications. Where technology has worked it has improved the quality of education more than almost any of the other changes by drawing in a wide range of children, and teaching skills. There are now some extremely good technology courses run exactly as Lady Parkes intended by staff drawn from a variety of subjects, but the final battle remains to be won, as the current debate demonstrates.

The account I have given indicates the breadth of consensus there was about the thrust to make technology a modern relevant subject rather than a regeneration of limited craft skills. That consensus significantly did not include some of those who are now in the forefront of criticism, and who have to an extent bided their time until problems which relate in essence to resources and training have surfaced.

The inevitable consequence of parsimony has been to force schools to concentrate on the cheaper attainment targets – planning and assessing, not the actual doing and making. How pointless it all becomes when the key activity is omitted or emasculated on cost grounds. The same is true if training is inadequate.

Technology was a new revolutionary subject, instilling panic in the ranks, but there was too little investment compounded by divisions within local education authority advisers and HMI. The orders were less developed than in other subjects: their limitations were acknowledged and the need for goodwill from teachers and schools recognised. It would have been desirable to have been more specific about the skills, to have emphasised the links with business knowledge, and to have modified the programmes of study for primary schools. The state of play and the extreme time constraints precluded this. Revolution patently needed to be followed by evolution. The key lay in training, interpreting, expanding, modifying, and applying common sense. This did not really happen and there are many to share the blame. It is for this reason, and remembering earlier reactions, that HMI reports have to be read with caution and set against direct experience in schools.

The subject baronies which were challenged may well have conspired to make the progress less smooth than it might have been. Subjects are a means, not an end, but technology and TVEI (the Technical and Vocational Education Initiative in schools) have faced the same difficulties. Delivering technology throughout the core subjects and art remains a challenge.

Technology stands at the crossroads. Some of the criticisms are less than disinterested. Ministers will need to have the courage to stand back and analyse the motives of the critics who have seized on the problems and ignored the potential. They must in the end make up their minds whether they want to let technology survive as an exciting concept or succumb to the pressure groups. They will also have to dig into their pockets. Technology is the litmus test for the national curriculum as a whole.

Technology was joined by modern languages in the extended national curriculum core to be taught to all children up to 16, an indication of the government's concern at the persistent failure of the population at large to learn any language other than its own, and some children were not very good at that!

There was initial concern that introducing a compulsory modern language for all children of all abilities for the first time would cause considerable teaching and resource difficulties and there were obvious caveats about 16-year-olds who would not be taking a language GCSE. Some language teachers seemed keen to preserve the elitist flavour of their subject: no other group claims that its subject is unsuitable for the less able. In the event, there was little real debate about the proposals from the working group chaired by Martin Harris, vice-chancellor of Essex University.

The Secretary of State, in an order in October 1989, had proposed that schools should be able to choose from two language lists: schedule 1 of eight working European Community languages; schedule 2 of eleven other languages of commercial and cultural importance. Many people felt that the format made the schedule 2 languages appear second class. In the interim and final reports to MacGregor in February and July 1990 the group proposed one consolidated list but said that if only one language was to be taught it would have to be from the EC. Where two languages were being studied they could come from outside the community and a pupil could choose either. It was a neat, acceptable solution.

The working group proposed four attainment targets which required the ability to understand spoken languages of various kinds and to respond appropriately though not necessarily orally; to express oneself effectively in speech and conversation; to read, understand, and respond appropriately to written language of various kinds; and to formulate, record, and convey meaning in the written language being studied.

MacGregor accepted the report although he did have reservations about four separate attainment targets each being given the status of a profile component. The NCC welcomed the report which was supported by the consultation. The final orders were simplified by the council to become listening, speaking, reading and writing, and the number of statements of attainment were reduced from 144 to 102, a clear example of NCC's ability to cut out unnecessary overlap within a subject and to remove jargon which was so abhorred by ministers.

When Kenneth Baker said that all children aged 11 and over would have to learn a modern language he was immediately attacked by the enthusiasts for limiting it to one. He reasonably pointed out that to make one compulsory was a major step and of course children who wanted to do more could. The need to provide space for a second or even third language was one of the pressing reasons for reducing the national curriculum for 14- to 16-year-olds.

6

A TIME AND A PLACE FOR EVERYTHING

History proved what the critics of the legal status of the national curriculum had always feared: a Secretary of State could change it to suit his own preferences which would not necessarily always be as benign as Kenneth Baker's insistence that primary school children should learn poetry by heart. When it came to history, the longest running saga in the national curriculum, Kenneth Clarke simply cut the bits he did not like.

History was always likely to be contentious and it more than lived up to the early promise. Queen Mary said that when she died Calais would be engraved on her heart. History will be on mine. Despite the early difficulties over mathematics, the debate over single and dual science and the arguments about grammar in English, the national curriculum had been introduced in a reasonably ordered fashion. When it came to deciding what children should know at 7, 11, 14, and 16 in mathematics and science, the attainment targets and programmes of study were the easiest to define. NCC moved into deeper waters in English but managed to keep its head above the surface. History and geography took the working groups and the council into quite different territory.

Ministers, civil servants, HMI and NCC acknowledged from the beginning that history would be fraught with difficulties. The council consoled itself with the fact that it had now gained considerable competence in the mechanics of the national curriculum's attainment targets and programmes of study. This was not to prove much consolation. Apart from being endless, any list of what a child should know would almost certainly be affected by personal choice and prejudice. Both history and geography had considerable political overtones, and if there was to be an invasion of the national curriculum for political purposes history and geography were the natural targets. The battleground was set.

There was the second but equally important problem of how history and geography should be taught. Was the basis of teaching to be facts or concepts? History was already riven by the argument over empathy, a concept which required children to imagine what it would have been like to live through a particular event or be alive at a particular time. They would be asked to describe, for example, the Battle of Hastings from a Norman soldier's point of view, what it was like to have been an Indian child at the time of American independence, or to have fought in the Vietnam war. Unintentional or not, empathy immediately ran children and teachers into political debate.

The use of empathy is, like everything else, a question of balance. It is self-evident that if children can get under the skin of the people they are studying they will have a better understanding of historical events, but they also need an understanding of chronology and the facts surrounding any given event. Empathy was typical of the reforms of education in the 1970s and 1980s that were fine in themselves but were counter-productive if taken too far.

In history the teaching of factual knowledge was pushed further and further into the background. Children no longer had to learn lists of significant events. The feeling amongst ministers, and some historians, was that history had lost its backbone.

The argument in favour of the new teaching methods was very similar to that used in English about the teaching of grammar. If children were taught investigational skills and encouraged to work from real evidence such as original documents and old buildings, they would find things out for themselves and would, therefore, remember them more clearly. This had much to commend it, not least the intelligent use of original documents. It did, however, inevitably lead to a concentration on local history, in itself perfectly respectable as children have to begin from somewhere – but history cannot stop at the doorstep. So when the national curriculum was proposed in 1988 history syllabuses consisted largely of local history, where the evidence was more readily available, the study of documents, dramatisation, and relied heavily on empathy. There was much for the working group and NCC to do.

The history working group also had to contend with the fact that, after poetry, history was Kenneth Baker's favourite subject. He was well-briefed and was sympathetic to the right-wing view that as it was being taught, school history paid too little attention to Britain's own history and heritage, that it had almost become anti-patriotic as people strived to become objective. While history has to be objective, there was evidence that children were not taught about Britain's past. Even worse was the evidence of HMI that history and geography had largely disappeared from primary schools apart from some peripheral involvement in topic work, such as the Tower of London or the Vikings.

In setting up the history working group in January 1989, Baker said:

> The programmes of study should have at the core the history of Britain, the record of its past and, in particular, its political, constitutional and cultural heritage . . . They should take account of Britain's evolution and its changing role as a European, Commonwealth and world power, influencing, and being influenced by, ideas, movements and events elsewhere in the world. They should also recognise and develop an awareness of the impact of classical civilisations.

The nearest he came to criticising the existing teaching methods was to say that the new lessons should foster a sense of place and time; a grasp of chronology and historical techniques; and the capacity for historical understanding based on sound evidence.

The working group, and subsequently NCC and ministers, would have to face up to the question of balance. How, for example, was the working group to treat the European Community? It could hardly be excluded, yet Mrs Thatcher, the first and most ardent of the Euro-sceptics, had made it known that she would be keeping a close eye on the syllabus. Therefore ministers and officials took great care over the choice of members to make sure there was a wide spread of interests from education and industry. They did not want pressure groups operating within the working group or to end up with a report which would cause political embarrassment as had happened with mathematics and English. The appointment of Commander Michael Saunders Watson, a former chairman of the Heritage Education Trust and owner of Rockingham Castle in Northamptonshire, to chair the group was extraordinary. He appeared to be an eccentric choice inspired by Baker after the two men had met at a reception and found they had a mutual interest in history. Saunders Watson's only obvious credentials were that he ran a stately home which was used by many schools and as a result had a keen but practical interest in history and education. He appeared to everybody to be a peculiarly Tory choice and looked to many as the first overt political appointment. Everybody feared the worst and characterised him as a right-wing amateur who would follow the party line. He went on to be a great disappointment to Mrs Thatcher and the right wing and a great but welcome surprise to history teachers.

The working group was soon into very considerable difficulty as it decided that it would not be possible to have attainment targets based on facts in any rational way. Like it or not the attainment targets would have to be based on skills of interpretation and critical awareness. The interim report sent to Baker in June 1989 recommended that the programmes of study should embrace the body of historical knowledge while the attainment targets should specify understanding and skills. This became the nub of the argument, but few outsiders could understand what the fuss was about. Politicians saw attainment targets which set specific goals as more important than programmes of study which put the flesh on the bones. Both are statutory, but the suspicions of ministers were aroused unless facts were not specifically included within the attainment targets. This was the symbol: the real battle was the deeper one of facts versus skills.

Baker was very concerned and unhappy with the report while Saunders Watson was unfazed. He took the common-sense view that what Baker wanted was not possible. If the five or so targets were based on facts, somebody would have to select the facts. In rare idle moments at the National Curriculum Council the staff would try to guess how Margaret Thatcher's list of facts would compare with Neil Kinnock's. The history working group did make an attempt to compile a working list but the attempt only went to show how impossible the task was. Baker called Saunders Watson to his office to tell him that the working group would have to revise its thinking and include more facts in the attainment targets. Like many men of his background Saunders Watson made it perfectly clear that while he would not deliberately rock the boat he was not prepared to be pushed around.

MacGregor replaced Baker only a matter of days before the interim report was published and said he welcomed the inclusion of historical knowledge in the programmes of study but told the working group:

> I doubt whether this approach puts sufficient emphasis on the importance of acquiring such knowledge and in ensuring that knowledge can be assessed. It runs the risk that pupils' grasp of the substance of history will not be clearly established or assessed . . . I am not convinced that the case has been made for knowledge remaining only in the programmes of study.

MacGregor asked the group to look again at ways of including essential historical knowledge in the attainment targets. He also wanted the final report to contain more chronology and for secondary school children to spend more time studying British history, which in the report had been given less than half the syllabus. The working group was also criticised for not addressing the twentieth century properly by almost entirely avoiding Hitler's part in the Second World War, with no mention of the Holocaust. NCC's view was that whatever was missing could be inserted during the consultation period. Other problems were not so easily dealt with. The interim report made history a public debate and yet again the national curriculum was in jeopardy.

With the publication of the interim report it was decided that the time was now right for the council and the working group to have official contact, which became the convention for subsequent subjects. Saunders Watson and members of the group came reluctantly to York. He said he could only stay for an hour and sat down in the conference room opposite members of the council with an official on either side of him. He initially turned down a suggestion that he and I should talk privately to get to know each other, but he came to realise that the council was not ill-disposed towards the working group and might even be able to help. When it came to the buffet lunch, we slid along a table together filling our plates and exchanging notes out of the corners of our mouths. The after-noon session began on a cordial note which surprised the two officials who had guarded him so carefully. We agreed to keep in touch and went on to become good friends.

Following the interim report, various interest groups began to battle over the reforms and it looked as if history would end in failure. In the final report the working group stood by the fundamental findings of the interim report which had caused such concern to ministers. There were many good detailed refinements and, in an attempt to satisfy ministers, almost too many facts were included in the programmes of study, but when it came to the basic principle nothing had been altered, indeed little could be altered as the working group's conclusions were unarguable. A knowledge of facts does not equal a knowledge and understanding of history.

MacGregor sat on the report for two months before publishing it in April 1990. The council knew that things were very seriously adrift if only because intended deadlines came and went. MacGregor was in a very difficult political position as Margaret Thatcher was determined to have her say in the final proposals. All the working group reports went to Downing Street for approval before they could be published and Mrs Thatcher was not going to approve history as it stood. In her eyes, Saunders Watson had gone native and the working group had let the country down. It seemed that she was determined that history was going to be the way she wanted it, based entirely on facts. Anything else was too soft and woolly.

History was rescued from limbo by Nick Stuart, the deputy secretary at the department who was responsible for the national curriculum. He realised that the report was in danger of being rejected and that if this happened there would be a real threat to the future of the government's flagship reform. He realised that there was no quick solution but thought a cooling-off period might offer MacGregor a reasonable opportunity of finding a way out of the impasse. With a little more thinking time the government might also come to see that there was no malice in the history working group and that there was a genuine problem.

It was proposed that MacGregor should publish the report and announce that he would conduct his own investigation into history. The justification was that the working groups reported to the Secretary of State and that he was, therefore, entitled to amend their reports in any way he chose. Saunders Watson accepted the proposal rather than see his report rejected without the working group's views having been published. The views were strong. The group warned that there was a very real danger of history being taken over as a propaganda weapon:

> Many people have expressed deep concern that school history will be used as propaganda; that governments of one political hue or another will try to subvert it for the purpose of indoctrination or social engineering. There will always be those who seek to impose a particular view of history through an interpretation of history.

The report also rejected Mrs Thatcher's request that there should be a greater emphasis on the learning and testing of historical facts: 'Names, dates and places provide only the starting points for understanding. Without understanding, history is reduced to parrot learning and assessment to a parlour memory game.'

The programmes of study in the final report were overloaded to a great extent with plenty of facts and the report stressed that essential and exemplary information should be a compulsory part of specific courses. The working group argued that children would only be able to show an understanding of history, which could be tested, if the relevant facts were learned. It was, therefore, unnecessary to test facts separately.

Writing to MacGregor, Saunders Watson said:

> We have given much thought to alternative methods of achieving our common objectives of ensuring that historial knowledge should be taught, learned and assesssed. We are convinced that the right way to achieve this is by placing specific historical information in the programmes of study, which have statutory weight, and assessing pupils' acquisition and understanding of that information through attainment targets which also have statutory weight.
>
> We have devised a way of doing so which is both flexible to operate, relatively simple to implement and allows some scope for freedom of choice.

Mrs Thatcher would have none of it.

Publication led to a major political row with Jack Straw, Labour's education spokesman at the time, accusing Mrs Thatcher of direct political interference:

> She tried to pack the working party with people she thought would back her. That did not work and she sent the report back. Now they [the government] are hoping the extra consultation will give them time to persuade people into thinking their way.

On the defensive, MacGregor said that nobody should be surprised that the prime minister had taken a strong interest in the subject. He said that history was so important that there should be a general public debate over several months before final proposals were published. He also asked

SEAC to report whether the testing methods suggested by the report were workable, and if not to suggest an alternative.

The next question that had to be resolved was who would undertake the work for MacGregor. Strictly speaking NCC should not have become involved because that would eventually lead to it consulting on a report which it had helped to write. Eric Bolton, the Senior Chief Inspector for HMI, was adamant that his inspectors could not do it for fear of damaging their independence. Civil servants would hardly be able to do the work on their own. The only acceptable solution was for the new report to be compiled nominally by the DES but it fell largely to Nick Tate, NCC's history officer, with help from myself (history is my own subject), the civil servants, and sotto voce from HMI, while there were many discussions with MacGregor.

Not only was Tate an excellent historian, he was also politically astute in a way the working group perhaps had not been when there had been an opportunity for compromise. He and I knew that the group's conclusion about the testing of facts was correct but that a new way had to be found of expressing that view. From containing too little, the working group had included too much but had still not gone far enough to meet demands for facts to be tested. Tate removed some of the things the working group had included and put back some of the things they had neglected. By some inspired rearrangement we persuaded MacGregor that while facts could not be included in the attainment targets they were none the less an integral part of the course. The new programmes of study were very demanding. They contained all that (and sometimes more than) any reasonable person could possibly want.

It is fair to say, however, that the biggest advantage we had was in the passing of time. It gave space for everybody to draw back and certainly the heat went out of the argument. MacGregor went out of his way to tell the right wing that their views would be listened to but that there would have to be a compromise. Our recommendations did include references to the teaching of facts, which seemed to placate the critics. MacGregor himself had come to accept the central premise over testing following advice from SEAC that the methods proposed by the working group offered a sound and workable basis for assessment.

In responding to the council's informal proposals in a long letter to me at the end of July, MacGregor felt it necessary to repeat that he had not made a formal response to the working group report in April because he wanted there to be a period of consultation in which there could be a thorough public debate on all the issues raised. He broadly accepted the proposals but offered his own solutions to resolve any remaining difficulties. His first change was to rename attainment target 1 as 'the knowledge and understanding of history' rather than the original definition of 'understanding history in its setting'. This, he said, was unclear and not sufficiently distinguished from attainment targets 2 and 3, 'understanding points of view and interpretations of history', and 'acquiring and evaluating historical information'. Attainment target 4, 'organising and communicating the results of historical study', would be assimilated into the remaining three targets. Strangely, he did not consider it necessary to adjust the statements of attainment which go to make up each attainment target. The crucial change, however, was to give 'the knowledge and understanding of history' a higher weighting so that it assumed more importance in the curriculum. NCC was also asked to produce new exemplary material for the statements of attainment, to provide a better overview of the twentieth century, including in particular the European Community, and to remove extraneous material and concentrate on content and essential information.

NCC – and Margaret Thatcher, more reluctantly – accepted MacGregor's proposals, and Tate and the council staff embarked on some high-speed work to meet all the demands. The final advice, based on the working group report but amended by MacGregor, went to his successor, Kenneth Clarke in December 1990. The council proposed three attainment targets to make up one profile component: 'knowledge and understanding', 'interpretation of history' and 'the use of historical sources'. Saunders Watson loyally subscribed to the proposals which were largely accepted by the consultation. Indeed, there were only 502 responses from schools and 168 from other organisations, although 48 per cent of those who replied were against the weighting of attainment target 1, and 47 per cent disagreed with the study content proposed for the half GCSE which could be taken in conjunction with a half course in geography. There was a feeling on all sides that a crisis had been avoided, that a reasonable balance had been achieved, and that honour had been satisfied.

The report assumed that history would encompass events taking place up to the present day, a position accepted both by Baker and MacGregor. In a letter to MacGregor with the final working group report, Saunders Watson said that lessons should be regularly reviewed: 'Recent events in China and Eastern Europe have lent added relevance to our work and reinforced our view that school history should be flexible enough to respond to changing circumstances and perspectives.' That view was never challenged until Kenneth Clarke entered the scene.

NCC made the grave mistake of relaxing and thinking that now history was at last in the bag, the national curriculum was unlikely to face any other major traumas. Its final report, based on the consultation but largely unchanged since it had been approved by MacGregor, sat on Clarke's desk. As the council was being praised for the work it had done, word came that Clarke had taken the gravest exception to history including present day events. That was not history, it was current affairs. Clarke, it appeared, was quite convinced that teachers could not be trusted to teach modern history in an even-handed way.

Quite contrary to normal practice Clarke had no discussions with NCC about history between the publication of its consultation document and the laying of statutory orders in March 1991. The decision on when the end date should be was not arrived at after seeking out the best advice or by involving the council in consultation, but was the result of a Dutch auction between Clarke and his officials as they gradually moved closer together. Clarke's opening bid was 1945. To their eternal credit the officials protested, pointing out that history, particularly twentieth-century history, had caused no end of difficulty for his predecessor and was now approved by the prime minister. There is no evidence to show that this had anything to do with anybody other than Clarke, and officials were concerned that any further tampering would rekindle the bitter debate we all thought had been successfully concluded.

The civil servants succeeded in moving him on from 1945 but they failed to persuade him that to put an artificial end to history was ludicrous and quite beyond the spirit of the history document. As Clarke and the officials went on with their haggling, the denouement of Communism was taking place. How could post-war history exclude that or the part President Kennedy played in East–West relations?

Clarke finally settled for a moveable feast. He decided that the period covered by modern history, studied by children aged from 14 to 16, should run from the turn of the century to a time 20 years before the present, with the cut-off point moving on in five-year periods. Whether or not it was a reasonable compromise, this was the first major and quite political intrusion into what was taught in the country's schools. And it should never have happened.

Even more disturbing is the fact that civil servants had to fight a gruelling battle to ensure he did not change a number of other things. His decision to allow children to drop history at 14 had led to complaints that they would learn little about the twentieth century and he therefore introduced a compulsory study unit on the Second World War for children aged 11 to 14 – but only after the council had made clear how unbalanced his decisions had made history become.

The timing of geography was staggered to start and finish slightly after history but, given the difficulties that surrounded history, it started second and finished first. Clearly there were rivalries between history and geography as they both realised that the working groups were their chance to secure the position of the two subjects in the curriculum as two of the foundation subjects. The geographers also had a score to settle with the scientists who in their view had stolen the earth sciences from them. The problem the geographers faced was that earth sciences had been done very well in the science document. NCC, using the wisdom of Solomon, said that as long as the earth sciences were taught coherently it did not matter whether they were part of geography or science.

The more serious immediate problem for the geography working group was the one it shared with history: the problem of facts in attainment targets. Was the curriculum to concentrate on capes and bays or was it to be about investigation and interpretation? Members of the group worked well together under the doughty chairmanship of Sir Leslie Fielding, vice-chancellor of Sussex University, and as far as one could see there were no internal tensions. They saw their remit as being perfectly clear: their task was to win the curriculum battle for geography. All that one heard was good news.

When the interim report was published in October 1989 it was a good one. The working group was buoyant but MacGregor was concerned that the seven attainment targets were well over the norm and against the trend of simplifying the statutory orders. His other misgiving was a mirror image of what was happening in history. The attainment targets were skill-based and not fact-based.

The third and very important isssue that surfaced with the interim report was the precise nature of geography, which was going to cause the greatest problems later on. It appeared to ministers that having lost earth sciences, the geographers were pushed into finding something else to put in its place. Partly because of the way geography teaching had moved in recent years and partly because the working group wanted to prove itself, the interim report turned out to be very heavily centred on political geography, economic geography, social geography and environmental geography. MacGregor, perhaps because he was under enormous pressure to show that he could stand up to the education professionals, became alarmed and argued that geography had moved away from its real purpose. Children should study the geography of their own country carefully and systematically, followed by European and world geography. By emphasising the alternatives the working group was losing sight of the basics.

There was particular concern about the environment. In submitting the interim report to MacGregor, Sir Leslie wrote: 'Environmental education is essential for today's children and geography should be the prime vehicle for it.' The government had always been sensitive to environmental issues and, while it welcomed the attainment target on the environment, there were considerable reservations behind the scenes and pressure was put on Sir Leslie to soften the tone of the report. Publicly MacGregor contented himself with voicing the council's own concern that environment should not become the exclusive possession of geography.

Continuing the pressure on putting knowledge before interpretation, MacGregor asked the working group to include knowledge in all the attainment targets. The government approved, for example, of the recommendation that a bright 7-year-old should know and be able to locate on a map of the British Isles the major relief features and rivers of the UK, including the Pennines, Lake District, Welsh Mountains, Scottish Highlands, and the rivers Severn, Thames and Trent.

When I met Sir Leslie after publication of the interim report he seemed concerned that the council was acting as the government's messenger. In a formal atmosphere in an office in the Education Department he removed his jacket to reveal large bright red braces, the most magnificent pair I have ever been privileged to behold. Somehow that set the scene and he soon realised that the council was as concerned as he was to ensure that the geography proposals were successful.

NCC advice was purely technical although it did express concern over the number of attainment targets and programmes of study. Geography and history are the best examples of what might have happened had the council been allowed to work alongside the subject group from the moment they were set up. It is quite possible that the problems caused by the size and political naïviety of the interim reports could have been avoided.

The working group, however, decided to stay with seven attainment targets, and to meet the government's demands for extra facts in the programmes of study while keeping everything they wanted. The geography working group, like history, was not going to be sold short. By the time of the final report it was clear that history – which was still to be finalised – and geography were going to be far too large to be accommodated in the school timetable. It was also clear that the working group was going to resist any suggestion that geography should become a half subject or that it should be paired with history. In his letter to MacGregor accompanying the final report, Sir Leslie was short and sharp and defensive only on teaching loads: 'We have resisted the temptation to include every aspect of this fascinating subject which would be of educational value.'

The seven attainment targets were now: 1, geographical skills; 2, the home area and region; 3, the UK within the European Community; 4, the wider world; 5, physical geography; 6, human geography; and 7, environmental geography. As the council began work on its own response to the final report MacGregor let it be known that the wording of the attainment targets would have to reflect more traditional geography and should not sound too sociological, environmental or political.

The council hoped that the consultation would show support for fewer attainment targets but that was not to be. Half supported the original seven attainment targets, while the remainder was split. Two-thirds of those who responded complained about the large number of statements of attainment, the price that was being paid for the inclusion of facts.

Council officers came to the conclusion that there should be three attainment targets. The civil servants opposed the proposal saying it was too radical and would not be supported by MacGregor. I argued that three attainment targets were more logical and would not harm the content or rigour of geography. Furthermore, anything over three would damage the whole symmetry of the national curriculum as it was now shaping.

MacGregor finally decided that while he accepted NCC's argument it was politically not possible for a Secretary of State to move so radically as from seven to three but that he would settle for five. There were no particularly obvious educational arguments for five so NCC then pointed out that if three were not politically acceptable it would be as well to stay with seven which were logically supported. As the argument continued, MacGregor's determination, as is often the way with ministers, hardened.

For the first and only time the officers prepared three separate proposals for the council members to consider, based on three, five, and seven attainment targets. The officers supported the three-target option but the debate was settled on political lines. I think that members, while not in the hands of the minister, felt insecure and the consultation advice had not given clear preferences. The rationale for staying with five not three attainment targets was developed along the lines that physical, human and environmental geography were important and distinct elements. The original attainment targets 2, 3, and 4 were combined as 'knowledge and understanding of places'. The attainment targets would be grouped into three profile components: geographical skills, places, people and environments. The council also recommended that the number of statements of attainment be reduced from 269 to 211 through eliminating overlap, although more ruthless pruning could have reduced the number to nearer 170. Officers and, no doubt, teachers felt somewhat frustrated.

The council's consultation report was sent to Clarke in November 1990 when he had been Secretary of State for six days: 'Council is recommending some changes to the proposals made by your predecessor. These are intended to make the geography curriculum more readily practicable in schools of all types whilst preserving the rigour of the original proposals.'

As in history, Clarke had no discussions with the council before announcing his decisions on geography. He prononouced on both subjects on the same day and took the opportunity to stress that he believed facts were more important than opinion. Announcing his decisions on geography, he said:

> I was not persuaded by those who argued that greater emphasis should be placed on the study of people's views and attitudes on geographical topics. I recognise that geography lessons will deal with conflicting opinions and attitudes on a number of questions, especially those concerned with human and environmental geography. Of course I am not opposed to pupils forming their own opinions – but I want those opinions to be soundly based.

He reintroduced items concerning ecological issues relating to the differing uses of land and how they affect scenic beauty but refused to allow a separate statement of attainment covering skills such as being able to use reference and recording systems. Both decisions were revealing.

The ecological issue showed the government's dilemma. In rapid succession ministers were against the proposals because they were worried about expense and the possibility of encouraging pressure groups, and for them because of the growing public interest in green issues and forthcoming regulations from the European Community. As regards skills, the message was constant: knowledge first and knowledge last. It was increasingly hard work to achieve a sensible balance.

In addition to their political difficulties, the geography and history reports also showed that subject-based working groups were getting out of hand and if ever there was an oppportunity to rein them in, MacGregor lost it over geography and history. By this time there was probably sufficient knowledge of how the system worked for specific guidance on attainment targets at least to have been drafted for the working groups and for much more precise remits. In the case of history this might have revealed the problems more directly to ministers at an earlier stage and have saved a lot of time and pain. There was, too, an argument for having different types of working groups with cross-subject representation and fewer members committed to subject lobbies. As it was, while beginning to lament complexity and over-prescription, ministers did nothing to prevent it continuing. Perhaps they felt that in fairness all subjects had to be seen to be approached in a similar way.

The council asked the history and geography working groups to bear each other in mind when they came to produce their reports and both resolutely failed to do so. Both were asked to provide programmes for a short course. Again, they failed to do so. Their half courses were nearer to nine-tenths.

The behaviour of MacGregor and particularly Clarke over history and geography raises the serious question of the role of ministers in the curriculum and the dilemmas caused when politics clash with educational needs. Until then MacGregor had followed Baker's example of seeing the main role of the Secretary of State as laying down policy and not becoming involved in professional matters.

It will not be possible to lay down clear dividing lines. Attainment targets and programmes of study are legitimate areas for politicians in the sense that they are, after all, part of the law of the land, but there is a need for great sensitivity all round when their views conflict with sound educational considerations. The question of detailed lessons and how they should be taught is not, I believe, one for ministerial intervention.

7

A MERRY DANCE

When the National Curriculum Council was first formed members were concerned that it would be some time before art, music, and physical education would be tackled. Members feared that schools might be tempted to ignore all three because when they were eventually introduced there would be no room for them in the timetable. There was also the problem that Baker's ten foundation subjects did not include drama and dance, both of which were flourishing in many schools.

The council called a meeting of people involved with art, music and PE to discuss the various issues raised before the working groups were set up, despite opposition from the DES which said that it was not NCC's concern. At the meeting the council said that the three subjects should hang together or be hanged together but the warning was ignored and the meeting was characterised by an argument over who owned dance. The one claim that was news to me was that dance belonged to art in just the same way as painting.

While the subject lobbyists argued amongst themselves, there was much behind the scenes debate, not to say confusion, before the art, music and PE working groups were set up. The fundamental argument centred on how many working groups there should be. Should there be one group to cover all three, one for art and music with a separate group for PE, one group with three sub-committees, or should there be one for each subject? The only real arguments for joint working groups was that in practice in schools they tended to be lumped together in what space there remained in the timetable, and that if the subject groups worked together they might see the need to limit their ambitions. The experience of NCC's conference indicated that this would be unlikely. From that point, however, the officers of the council had an excellent working relationship with each of the different groups.

For the first time I was frequently asked for my views, both by MacGregor and his officials, even to the point of suggesting people who might be asked to serve on the working groups. As to how many working groups there should be, I could only say that I saw reason on all sides. The arguments that won the day were that it would look very bad if the subjects were not treated separately and that as the three subjects had little in common they might end up destroying each other.

Once it had been resolved that there should be three working groups it had then to be decided the type of reports they should prepare, as it had been agreed that the attainment targets and programmes of study in art, music and PE would not be as detailed as those of the other subjects. The working groups could be seen as being lucky in not being so circumscribed, with the freedom that would bring, or as downgraded without the full influence of the earlier groups.

Sadly, if understandably, the groups did not take the view that they would be better placed with fewer constraints. They wanted to be as detailed and as broad-ranging as mathematics and science, with equality in the pecking order. These subjects have always felt that they were seen as of lower importance than the rest of the curriculum. Their feelings were not unjustified. When it came to appointing NCC officers for art, music and PE the DES suggested that they should be a salary grade lower than 'academic' staff.

In setting up the music and PE working groups, MacGregor went for a sprinkling of minor celebrities. Mike Batt, the popular music composer, was appointed to serve on the music working group under the chairmanship of Sir John Manduell, principal of the Royal Northern College of music. The PE chairman, Ian Beer, headmaster of Harrow and a former English rugger international, was joined by Steve Ovett, the runner and Justin Fashanu, the footballer, neither of whom played a major part in the deliberations. The government's final and controversial decision was to put dance within PE which was to prove a mixture of triumph and disappointment.

As the three working groups began there was considerable uncertainty about the status of their subjects as MacGregor had already said that he was considering making art, music and PE optional at 14. He went through a stage when he believed they could be dealt with in after-school activities. He certainly thought that PE could be dropped as it was ideally suited to after-school games, which might work for the independent schools but would not in the majority of state schools where teachers were already complaining of over work.

The PE working group was delightful. Ian Beer, who was about to retire, was not going to be diverted by anybody: ministers, civil servants, the teachers, or even the National Curriculum Council. He and I met in the Caledonian Club shortly after he had been appointed. During lunch I mentioned that I was rather proud that Scotland had won the grand slam the year before and in return he said that when he had played for England in 1954 he had scored the winning try at Twickenham, which deprived Scotland of the Triple Crown. As we retired to the smoking room, Beer fell back with a huge roar and accused me of luring him to the Caledonian Club to humiliate him, for as he walked into the room he was faced with two massive canvases depicting the Scottish Grand Slams of 1984 and 1990.

In discussing the working group, Beer said he was very unhappy that officials had told him that the working group could not recommend that every child should be taught to swim. He said that if the group came to that conclusion, he would not delete it, and did not. He was also astounded at what had happened to PE teaching in recent years in terms of jargon and obscurity and the move against practice and towards theory; that it was better to take a degree in how to run round the track than to run round it. He was, however, perfectly enlightened about the breadth of sport and happily embraced dance without any encouragement from the council: 'I have often thought that if the England forwards had been taught dance we might have been able to jink past a few more Aussies.'

Beer was also clear about the reality of MacGregor's contention that PE could largely be handled in after-school activities. While independent schools could fulfil what MacGregor wanted, most state schools could not. He knew more than enough about comprehensive schools and he was looking for genuine solutions.

In the interim report, the working group said that it was disappointed by the lower status that was apparently being given to PE, along with art and music. The group expressed their concern at suggestions that PE should not necessarily be compulsory at 14 as the physical development of young people should not be left to chance and hoped that the government would accept the advice of the National Curriculum Council that it should be compulsory for all children. The report also recommended that all children should learn to swim by the time they were 11 and that they should have at least one residential experience as part of their outdoor education.

Kenneth Clarke's reply was not enthusiastic. He rejected the group's proposal for three attainment targets: 'planning and composing' (designing specific displays in, for example, gymnastics or dance); 'participating and performing'; 'appreciating and evaluation'. He said he was not convinced this was the right structure for an essentially active subject and proposed one attainment target based on performance. Beer was crestfallen when he went on to read: 'I recognise that the group wishes to avoid using jargon . . . I am afraid that I am not convinced that you have succeeded in your aim. I do not consider that the words used in your attainment targets are satisfactory.'

The working group was given no indication that PE would be compulsory for all and also received a dusty response to its swimming proposals: 'This and other recommmendations would have serious practical implications . . . It is no part of the group's remit to make resource recommendations . . . they must be realistically related to what is available.'

Clarke's somewhat brutal response contrasted starkly with those of Baker and MacGregor who recognised that the working groups were made up of volunteers who were frequently distinguished people in their own right. NCC was told by the Education Department to ask the working group to cut back on the report but did not feel this was appropriate and suggested only technical improvements.

Since my first meeting with Beer, the council had a very constructive relationship with the working group. The final recommendations were published after I had left NCC, but ironically I felt it was the first time that it had been of real help to a working group, yet nobody could say it had sought to change its views.

The report was launched in August 1991 at Lancashire County Cricket Club's Old Trafford headquarters by Robert Atkins the then sports minister who had been moved into the Education Department from Environment. The working group refused to give way on swimming but did concede the arguments on the number of attainment targets and jargon. Clarke defused the swimming proposals by saying that his department would carry out a survey of swimming facilities in order to judge how quickly swimming tuition could be made compulsory in primary schools. Local education authorities have now been given until August 1994 to introduce the necessary swimming lessons to ensure that all children in state schools can swim by the time they are 11.

Atkins initially shared Beer's enthusiasm for dance, saying that Fred Astaire would have made a first class cricketer given 'his marvellous footwork'. He appeared to have changed his mind when he told *The Times Educational Supplement*: 'I think there is a possibility of dance as a cop-out, the sixth form disco as substitute for physical activity. I don't think I agree with that.'

After consultation, NCC rejected the group's view that dance should be compulsory up to 16 as it was persuaded by the all-boys schools, mostly independent, that it was not feasible to ask large teenage boys to take dance seriously if they did not want to. The dancers Wayne Sleep and Anthony Dowell joined a campaign to persuade Clarke to change his mind.

Lord Palumbo, chairman of the arts Council, criticised the council for disregarding the advice of professionals serving on the working group. He said:

arts education in England has an international reputation for the quality of experiences, its infrastructure and support. The implication of the [Mr Clarke's] orders will erode and set back the work developed in music and dance over the past 20 years.

While the PE working group had shown an awareness of the needs of the whole curriculum, the art working group appeared to give credence to the widely held belief that the teachers who are least able to cross boundaries and work with other people are to be found in art departments throughout the country. Within their own subject they are very often liberal in their approach, but when challenged they can become very defensive.

Understandably the art working group was upset at having lost design to technology and it had a point as ministers never grasped that the best design work within CDT was frequently carried out in art courses. The group was particularly aggrieved that art was not going to be compulsory throughout the curriculum. The group thought that this would lead to a loss of status of the subject in the school because they believed it would lead to a reduction in the number of children who would take GCSEs and A-levels, examinations which in the past had secured the standing of art in the timetable. The working group turned in on itself and nothing was known about their thinking or their proposals until the publication of the interim report. The practice had now developed whereby I wrote to the working group chairman after publication to suggest a meeting. The art working group chairman, Lord Renfrew, Master of Jesus College, Cambridge, replied to say that he was too busy. The council was rather taken aback by the response as it knew the advice it would offer would be helpful. In the face of continued refusals to agree to a meeting I wrote to Renfrew giving him the council's views on how the proposals could be simplified. He wrote a courteous letter of thanks.

NCC's final proposals on art and music were made after I had left it. In art, the three original attainment targets of 'study', 'understanding', and 'making and investigating', were cut to two: 'investigating and making', and 'knowledge and understanding'. All pupils should undertake a balanced programme of art, craft and design, work individually and in groups, use computers where possible, and work in two or three dimensions. The proposals for both subjects brought back memories of the English working group's ill-advised booklist when it, not the working group, published a list of recommended composers and artists. David Pascall, the new chairman, insisted that they were only examples. Perhaps he should have known better.

While I was at the council the view was that lists should be avoided. If there is a national curriculum which is largely statutory people are too easily confused into believing that all of it is legally required. Recommended artists included L. S. Lowry, Leonardo da Vinci, Henri Rousseau, George Stubbs and Elizabeth Frink.

The music working group was as annoyed as the PE and art working groups to be told that its subject would not be a complete subject and would not be compulsory after 14. While being aware of the constraints, the music group under Sir John Manduell did an outstanding job and was not inhibited by government action. The working group was more in touch with its subject in the widest sense than practically any of the others. Within music there are two kinds of people, those who believe music is for everybody and those who believe it should be traditional classic music. Manduell and his working group judged the temperature correctly and were talking of music for everybody. Manduell was a superb and diplomatic chairman as well as a congenial dinner companion.

In responding to the interim music report, Clarke said that he would prefer two attainment targets combining 'performing and composing', and 'listening and knowing' rather than the four proposed, and that it was biased towards children who were good instrumentalists or singers.

The final music report was good and unstuffy, but the role of NCC changed dramatically. By the time NCC began its consultation on music it had abandoned its commmittee structure so that when it came to offer advice to the Secretary of State it was fundamentally based on the views of the council members. It certainly was more difficult to rebut criticism that they were simply doing what they had been asked to do by the Secretary of State.

NCC can only claim to be truly independent if it can justify its views. It is as bad for ministers to seek to impose their views on the council as it is for teachers to claim that they have sole rights to the curriculum and that nobody else must tell them what to do. Genuine improvements can only be achieved when there is a clearly defined partnership in which people trust each other. NCC's report to Clarke following consultation on music was the first to ignore practically all the advice it received. The recommendations made significant changes to the original proposals and ignored the preferences of about half of those teachers and educationists who had given their views. Criticising the working group's proposals, the council said that many of the recommendations were difficult to understand and difficult to manage – particularly for primary school teachers. The changes it was proposing would ensure that all pupils had a basic grounding in art and music. While art and music would be compulsory only for pupils aged 5 to 14, schools would be expected to offer some lessons in music or art or a mixture of both to senior classes. To some this seemed little more than a pious hope.

In music, the working group's three attainment targets of 'performing', 'composing' and 'appraising' were reduced to two: 'performing and composing' and 'knowledge and understanding'. Teachers would decide the time given to each requirement. Throughout their school careers, pupils would be expected to work individually or in groups, use computers to create and record music, study European classical music from its earliest roots to the present day, and learn about music from the countries and regions of Britain and a variety of Western and non-Western cultures. It was a nice, if unintentional, contrast with PE. In effect the council was saying that knowing facts about music was more important than making it. Recommended composers included Lennon and McCartney, Fats Waller and Duke Ellington, Bach, Beethoven, Schubert, Stravinsky, Britten and Tippet: an arbitrary list with a hint of populism thrown in. The jazz-loving Secretary of State was delighted at the inclusion of Waller and Ellington.

The immediate reaction to the council's proposals from professional musicians was uproar. The protest was led by the conductor Simon Rattle whose legitimate contention was that a concentration on classical music and on listening rather than playing would turn children away from music. Initially, Clarke's response was to say that Rattle should read the report not press accounts of it. In a brilliant discourse on the BBC 2 *Late Show* Rattle revealed a more complete mastery of it than the Secretary of State.

In announcing his final proposals for art and music, Clarke said that he accepted that the subjects are and should remain essentially practical: 'The acquisition of knowledge and understanding should not be separated from the practical activities of making, performing, creating, looking and listening.' Clarke made a number of changes which he said he hoped would end the argument over the division between making music and learning about it and claimed that much of the argument was about packaging rather than substance. In reality Clarke achieved 90 per cent of what he wanted by going back 10 per cent from what his anxious-to-please NCC had told him, a neater solution than having to pull back a great deal more. It is unlikely, however, that any changes would have been made at all if it had not been for the intervention of Simon Rattle and later Sir John Manduell who expressed his own displeasure at what the council had done to the working group's proposals.

Art and music are the ultimate expressions of the government's determination to stress knowledge over understanding. MacGregor had made some concessions and Clarke had been forced to with history, but art and music allowed Clarke to reveal the pure streak that had existed in the beginning: knowledge was more important than skills. We live in an age where facts need more frequent updating than skills.

The controversy over the council's proposals for music showed the difficulty facing it if it could not provide evidence that its decisions were based on advice and consultation both with experts and the people who would be expected to teach the recommended subject lessons. When council decisions were announced those affected were entitled to ask by what right and what process that particular route had been chosen.

In order to ensure that NCC could offer credible advice I had decided from the beginning that the council should be more than its 15 or so members and formed a number of committees. Members worked with a range of people who brought in the outside world and specific skills to advise on individual subjects or issues. Civil servants were wary and initially found it difficult to cope with the uninhibited advice from volunteers with great professional competence and a lot of dedication. Members of the committees were not chosen to represent organisations or formal interests. They were acknowledged experts in their own areas, with solid practical experience. The council was of course free to ignore their advice but the committees did assist it by giving a disinterested view based on their own professional judgement.

The committee structure was very effective and did give NCC credibility when dealing with subject groups and ministers. Clarke, in particular, frequently asked NCC to justify its views and it became very important to be able to say that whatever was being challenged was not just the opinion of council members. In my last few months the council abolished these broadly based committees and set up member-only committees. This has created a situation in which it can appear that there is no liaison with anybody.

Art and music illustrated how vulnerable the council is if it does not have, and be seen to have, its own source of independent advice. When challenged on the art and music recommendations made to the Secretary of State, the council had to concede that they were based only on the views of its members, a classic example of what I had always feared.

One cynical rationale for the creation of the National Curriculum Council might be that it was very useful for a government to be able to seek advice from an independent body which would always tell the government what it wants to hear. If that advice provokes a strong reaction, as it did in music, the government can then distance itself from the independent body which is left to pick up the pieces.

8

THE NIGHTMARE OF KEY STAGE 4

The unhappy story of key stage 4 which lays down what children should be taught between 14 and 16 runs through the first three years of the National Curriculum Council's history, at first behind the scenes and then in the full glare of often acrimonious publicity.

From the very beginning the troubles that would build up for key stage 4 and the council were spotted by Peter Watkins, NCC's deputy chief executive. Nobody else involved had the foresight of Watkins, who had been the headmaster of two schools before moving to the School Curriculum Development Committee and was an acknowledged expert on secondary school organisation.

He first raised the problem of key stage 4 before NCC was formally in existence when we met together in a rented room in York to consider what were likely to be the main difficulties facing the introduction of the national curriculum. He singled out key stage 4 immediately. Watkins convinced me that day in June 1988 that whatever was done with the national curriculum, and however the problems were resolved, it would not be possible to teach all ten subjects in their entirety for children aged 14 to 16 unless everything else was excluded. He identified the basic problem which was that if the full national curriculum course was combined with GCSEs there would barely be room to cover the ten, let alone introduce subjects outside the compulsory curriculum, such as a second modern language, the classics, or economics.

Schools that wanted to combine the breadth and balance of the national curriculum, which by law had to be provided for all children up to 16, with other subjects would be faced with what Watkins regarded as logistically insuperable problems. Watkins and I then met with SEAC, the civil servants and HMI to raise the question of key stage 4. We received the most discourteous reception, the first indication that no matter how justified proposals were they would not get very far if they were out of tune with current official thinking. Indeed, there was likely to be unpleasantness and not just professional disagreement.

Key stage 4 was pushed more and more into the background on the basis that it would be a long time before the entire national curriculum would be introduced into schools. Watkins and I took the opposite view: the time gap gave us time to work out a rational solution. Secondary school heads shared our concerns, pointing out quite properly the long lead times which schools need if the curriculum is to change. Examinations to be sat in 1994 need courses to be introduced in 1992.

With the introduction of the local management of schools (LMS), heads were also under considerable staffing and financial pressures as they were being exhorted to shape their staff for the 1990s. Self-management was, for the first time, forcing state school heads to consider long-term planning and staffing into the future. They were asking fundamental questions such as will we need more teachers in music, art and PE, or will there have to be redundancies? At the same time they were coping with the introduction of mathematics, English, science and technology. Without clear answers, they could not begin to plan. Attempts Watkins and I made to force discussion of key stage 4 met with complaints that we were rocking the boat by questioning the fundamentals of something which was perfect in its origin. That these arguments were futile is proved by the fact that key stage 4 did become the major problem for the curriculum.

During Kenneth Baker's period in office I was virtually prevented from ever getting a real chance to talk to him alone about key stage 4 and when I did it was not possible to deal with the difficulties adequately. Towards the end of his time Baker was beginning to hear complaints from heads and he wanted to discuss the issues. While he acknowledged that key stage 4 would have to be dealt with, civil servants and HMI were apparently unconcerned.

HMI ought to have seen the difficulties that lay ahead and I suspect that they were going on an agenda of their own. Despite the growing anxieties of heads, it was initially difficult to get NCC concerned, partly because Education Department officials attempted to prevent discussion. Once it was on the agenda it was difficult to persuade the members to do very much more than acknowledge the problem, let alone take action. The Education Department adopted the approach of the ostrich. There were, of course, other concerns but there was no justification for the decision to do nothing in the hope that the problem would go away. Council officers were at that stage not offering solutions but identifying the difficulties that were stacking up ahead and suggesting that working parties or groups be set up to consider ways forward.

The first thing that had to be established with ministers was what if anything was immutable and where compromises, if required, could be made. One of the ironies was that throughout Baker's time no minister would contemplate a national curriculum which did not cover all the subjects until 16. There was no talk of even a limited extension to the core subjects of mathematics, English, and science. Any proposed solution would run into the immediate rock of the GCSE which ministers, teachers, and examiners considered to be untouchable, given the amount of time, money and effort that had been invested in its introduction, not to mention the fact that teachers were handling the courses rather well. The obvious solution to bring the GCSE into line with the national curriculum attainment targets was, therefore, ruled out. At that time too, SEAC had enough problems without contemplating major changes in the GCSEs, as it was already in dispute with the examination boards following Baker's request to cut back the number of GCSEs and other examinations to ensure that all courses were relevant and rigorous.

The conflict between the national curriculum and the GCSE falls into three parts: philosophical, content and organisational. National curriculum assessment is designed to give a map of attainment at specific points in a continuing process. The map makes clear, for example, whether a pupil is sharper in practical work than theory, or in written rather than oral communication. The GCSE results were reported through a simple grade and the examinations were terminal, a summation rather than a snapshot. National curriculum assessment is more in line with the developments in post-16 education and training where specific credits are achieved. Differences in content were considerable: reconciling them would be a laborious process involving a lot of negotiation. While there was much common ground in the core subjects, there were problems about English language and literature, the balanced dual award science and the three separate sciences. With other subjects, it became even harder.

Organisationally, the problem was that to take GCSEs in all ten subjects would have been a daunting task with no room for anything else. Although this was never seriously proposed, what were pupils to do? In history and geography, for example, there were only full GCSEs, the half course still had to be invented. Technology could not be delivered through craft design and technology or home economics. So was it GCSEs in some subjects which met attainment targets and national curriculum assessment in others? Could half-subject GCSEs be allowed? Would subject groups wear it?

As NCC came to consider the problems towards the end of 1989 I was saying privately that the radical solution would be to test 16-year-olds against the national curriculum levels of 1 to 10 rather than by making them sit GCSEs which graded from A to G. To have both was unnecessary. The courageous and logical thing to have done would have been to use the attainment targets as the yardstick. Apart from being more logical, that proposal would have been closer to what most people in industry required. They wanted to know what specific skills school leavers had and that is where the profile components would have come into their own. Records of achievement based on national curriculum attainment targets which made up each profile component in a subject would show, for example, which branches of mathematics or science a school leaver was good at. If teenagers were to be employed in a selling job the employer would want to know what their strengths were in written and spoken English. A GCSE grade does not tell an employer very much.

This was an unwelcome and radical solution and was probably one step too far. That was also the first time in my life when I was behaving like a good civil servant and not saying outside what I was saying inside. The suggestion was received with unnecessary hostility and not the rational discussion it would have been reasonable to expect from institutions as mature as the Education Department and HMI.

When the national curriculum comes to be reviewed in, say, 20 years, people will probably conclude that England and Wales would have had a much better state education system if there had been a radical reform of GCSE rather than the abandonment of key stage 4 and the broad and balanced curriculum the country had so painfully won for itself. The only concession was to regrade GCSEs from 10 to 1 with a grade 10 being slightly harder than the A grade it replaced.

The council grew more worried through 1989 and it became clear that the heads of independent schools were as aware of the problem as the heads of state schools, although their priorities were different. Independent schools wanted the three sciences and space for the extra subjects, particularly languages and the classics. Their solution from the start was that the national curriculum would have to be reduced in some way to enable them to fit in everything they wanted. They were deaf to the point that whatever the solution that was eventually decided for state schools it did not matter to them as they were not compelled to follow the national curriculum and could pick from it what they wanted. There was concern amongst the independent heads that they would have to take account of the reforms as they could be in competition with improved state schools and were particularly worried about the effect grant-maintained schools would have on their intake. They could, however, have followed the curriculum through to the age of 14 and then gone their own way while maintaining a say in the shape of GCSEs.

While independent heads maintained a united front and had considerable influence, state heads were divided and too often ignored by ministers. Some had sympathy with the idea that schools should offer a wide choice at 14 and 16 while others thought that a homogeneous curriculum of ten subjects up to 16 was probably broad enough. Children could add their other subjects later.

The red letter day came in the summer of 1989 at a meeting with civil servants, SEAC, and Eric Bolton, the Senior Chief HMI. Top of the agenda was key stage 4! Watkins and I looked at each other and burst out laughing. It was a bitter sweet moment of vindication: the problem had now been recognised but too much time had been lost. From then on there was not a meeting of a general nature that did not have key stage 4 on the agenda. The change of heart had come about following the persistence of Watkins and myself, pressure from the independent heads and, importantly, the growing realisation in SEAC that full GCSE courses in all ten subjects would be insupportable.

At last we had got through to people that key stage 4 was an unmitigated disaster. Civil servants said that I should see John MacGregor, the new Secretary of State, as soon as possible to brief him on the mounting difficulties. Baker had apparently told MacGregor of my concerns and that there was an agreement that I should have access to ministers, a convention MacGregor was happy to continue. I spent a long time with him in his room at the Education Department going through key stage 4 as fairly as I could, making the main points. He knew by the end of that meeting that he had a problem which could blow up in his face and that it had to be solved. His trust in NCC was unreserved and he said that it should be entrusted with finding the solutions. He explained that he was under pressure from the independent schools while admitting it was illogical that they should have such a powerful voice in the national curriculum. Even at that first meeting I sensed that he was insecure about his own position – although not as insecure as he was to become – and that he had to guard his flank.

SEAC began to propose half courses in some subjects and combination GCSEs in others. While the relations between the two councils were soundly based, despite what the critics were saying, NCC officers and members had growing reservations about the GCSE and saw that it would have to be changed and adapted although it was agreed that to suggest abandoning it was too ambitious. For its part, SEAC, which was experiencing great difficulties over the standard assessment tasks for 7-year-olds, felt that it had to defend the position of the GCSE and to some extent the exam boards.

There was, however, a discernible shift of opinion among some ministers. I had begun at this time to see more of Angela Rumbold, the Minister of State, and she had growing reservations about the terminal feel of GCSE, believing that there should be continuity. She was beginning to think about the academic vocational divide. Rumbold, more than Tim Eggar, her successor, deserves credit for the move towards courses based on credits and modules, in which pupils could build up their own portfolio by studying a series of short courses. She was beginning to see that while it would be politically difficult, there might be an argument for a substantial revision of GCSE. She appreciated that there should be continuity at 16 and recognised that attainment targets might be a better measure of pupils' performance at least in some subjects. Rumbold was not enamoured of the independent schools, whose perception of the average child was one who could take 12 O-levels, as she had more of a feeling for what the majority of children would go through in their schooling. The people who would want to cram in extra subjects comprised only around 5 per cent of the school population.

The over-large history and geography orders simply illuminated and added to the problem. A deal would have to be struck between the two subjects. It was perfectly clear that a government which was not resourcing anything adequately in education was hardly likely to resource every school to provide every subject as a full course, even if room could be found. History and geography could be combined in a modular way over two years with two modules for each being taught alternately, which would satisfy the demands of the national curriculum. SEAC countered by arguing that the law required terminal examinations at the end of each key stage and that modules could not be tested or validated. NCC said that this was a problem to be solved, not accepted, and that it was quite possible to limit the number of modules and impose safeguards to standards. North of the border modules were working well and it did not seem necessary to have full courses in every subject. Others could be combined in some way.

The other solution was simply to say that at 14 children could, with certain exceptions, choose what they wanted to study. I believed then and believe now that this would be turning our backs on the benefits of the national curriculum. A country whose state education service had been bedevilled by patchiness and a lack of entitlement had at last got itself a national curriculum which it should hang on to at all costs while finding compromises within it. The national curriculum would ensure that all children would have a core of subjects up to 16 to which they could later add.

The first piece of my thinking which I shared with Angela Rumbold, and which she enthusiastically endorsed, was that there were only five subjects which should remain untouchable up to 16 and that became the extended core, with technology and the modern language added to mathematics, English and science. With the pressure of the single European market and the frequent calls by ministers for children to learn modern languages, which had been one of the country's failures, it was unthinkable that they could go back on that. Rumbold was also extremely keen on technology. She was considered to be right wing but was very enlightened when it came to education. Unlike some other ministers, she knew what made schools tick. She knew what technology was, she knew schools would have to change, and she knew girls would benefit from it. She was also close to Margaret Thatcher and told me that the prime minister was happy with the approach of the extended core

A story was leaked to *The Times* which indicated Rumbold's thinking at the end of 1989. The government was considering making some subjects in the national curriculum optional, cutting back on others and by-passing GCSE courses for 14- to 16-year-olds. The first suggestion of the extended core appeared at this time with the government indicating that all children up to 16 would have to study mathematics, English and science, and that a modern language and technology might also be added to the list. Rumbold was clearly thinking that the national curriculum, which went from level 1 to level 10 and covered the whole of a child's school career, could be used to measure a child's performance rather than rely on the GCSE. She was thinking that children at 14 might be able to drop history, geography, art, music and physical education if they reached level 8. She was setting her sights very high and in the event levels were dropped for art, music and PE. An unnamed minister told *The Times*: 'It is quite apparent that at 14 something is going to have to give for some children.'

MacGregor, however, gave no hints as to the way he was thinking and the council believed that it was still working within the constraints of a ten-subject curriculum. The civil servants became aware that the council and myself were increasingly likely to defend the national curriculum up to 16 so that there was a compulsory element to every subject even if compromises had to be made. The task was to look for workable solutions rather than to abandon parts of the national curriculum. In considering technology, for example, the council made several suggestions. If it was not to be a whole subject for all children it could be combined as a half subject with others, such as art or economics, all of which was legitimate.

MacGregor was hearing other voices. Independent schools were very powerful and influenced ministers and civil servants towards cutting back the compulsory requirements of the curriculum. In tandem, HMI saw their chance to rein in the national curriculum and argued that at 14 children should have more choice than the curriculum would allow. HMI saw the opportunity to remove a huge part of the curriculum with the reform of key stage 4 and returned to trying to convince ministers that too much prescription was undesirable.

State education in England and Wales was in danger of going full circle: a government that had introduced the national curriculum to ensure that there was a uniform curriculum across the country was now being told by its own inspectors that it was over-prescriptive, too detailed and too complex. MacGregor listened because he was so concerned about the overloading of teachers. Civil servants, HMI, and independent schools, with whom HMI would have few dealings, were taking the same line but for their own reasons.

As the end of the year approached, I learned that MacGregor was going to make a speech to the Society of Education Officers in January 1990. It also became clear that although he was listening to the council, he was probably going to be more influenced by the other voices. I would normally have been sent a draft of his speech for consultation before he delivered it. In this case I was not.

MacGregor telephoned me two nights before his conference appearance and told me what he was going to say and that he hoped I would go along with it. I told him with all the passion I could muster that he had got it wrong, he had been misinformed. Even if he did not want to go down the lines the council was favouring he should not close any doors. I felt I had been inadequately consulted and that the way this had happened was wrong. He was abashed about that but clearly the wheels had turned. It was an unhappy moment because MacGregor was under considerable pressure and felt that he had no alternative. We had a tense conversation during which I felt he would have liked to listen but could not afford to. My protestations were not going to make his decisions any easier.

MacGregor told the conference that some pupils would be able to drop certain subjects, that new GCSEs would be introduced in combined subjects and that half GCSEs might be taught in others. All pupils would have to take full GCSE courses in mathematics, science and English and would continue to study technology and a modern language until they were 16. In other subjects schools would be able to provide courses which did not come up to full GCSE standards but would meet national curriculum requirements. He said that he was also considering making PE optional as he believed that this could largely be achieved in after-school activities.

When bright children reached level 8 in the national curriculum, perhaps at 15, they would be able to continue with GCSE in other subjects such as the classics, a second modern language, or English literature. Technology would be compulsory up to 16 but MacGregor said he would ask the National Curriculum Council to consider suitable courses for children who achieved good GCSEs before they were 16. This proposal was backed by HMI, but it was administratively difficult to introduce. By the time a school knew who was going to get their GCSEs early it was going to be too late for the pupil to drop anything in time to gain any real advantage; also, pupils who were extremely good at a subject were likely to want to continue it rather than drop it. Nobody really understood the speech, but the principles that emerged were continuity, breadth and balance, and a flexibility which encapsulated the quart into a pint pot problem and what was to be done about it.

The council then set to work on the speech to offer the Secretary of State advice on the reform of key stage 4. The more work the council did, the more it became convinced of two things. One was that it was perfectly feasible to have the extended core contained in 70 per cent of available school teaching-time leaving a generous 30 per cent for the rest. The second was that that was what most schools wanted. When the council asked state school heads whether they really wanted art and music to be removed from the national curriculum they said they wanted a solution which kept the breadth and balance to 16. While this recognisably became the stance of NCC, the civil servants, HMI and the ministers were going the other way. MacGregor was being torn in different directions. NCC was put under pressure not to publish the guidance but insisted that the public should know what the present position was.

I had no interest in alienating MacGregor and Circular 10 on key stage 4 was finally published in May 1990 after the Education Department had seen as many as a dozen drafts. The circular was bland and did not set out to propose solutions. The council genuinely believed that MacGregor's speech needed to be explained against the aims and legal requirements of the curriculum. Key stage 4 was defined as the national curriculum of all ten foundation subjects plus religious education, additional subjects, and cross-curricular themes, skills and dimensions, such as citizenship, economic and industrial understanding, careers, personal health, and the environment.

Schools were advised that the 1988 Education Reform Act did not require children to study all subjects to the same depth and breadth. Pupils could select non-core foundation subjects for GCSE single-subject awards which would take about 10 per cent of curriculum time. Other subjects could be taken as part of combined GCSEs, or as separate subjects assessed under GCSE arrangements but not to the full breadth of a GCSE, for about 5 per cent of curriculum time.

In Circular 10, NCC said that everything possible should be done to ensure parity of esteem between the various courses. It also warned schools that a number of small blocks on the timetable would require skilful organisation if key stage 4 was to be implemented successfully. Many teachers might find it difficult to sustain pupil motivation from week to week. Fragmentation of the curriculum was a danger to be recognised. Courses that led only to a national curriculum level rather than a GCSE certificate might, at least initially, lack acceptance by employers. Teachers might find it difficult to achieve continuity and to sustain worthwhile contact between pupil and teacher. A solution, the council suggested, might lie in using different time-frames – for example, by using modules which provided relatively concentrated courses over a shorter period.

The council then embarked on six months' hard work and heard a variety of suggestions of varying quality before presenting its final advice to the Secretary of State. The final advice contained a number of possible solutions, but when I saw MacGregor before publication I proposed the most workable solution. The suggestion was that the extended core should take 60 per cent of the timetable, with 10 per cent divided between history or geography either as combined subjects or as single subjects, 10 per cent to art, music, and PE to be divided as the school decided, and 5 per cent to religious, personal and social education, which would leave 15 per cent for other subjects. This was the 70/30 solution.

The final document contained a number of solutions and MacGregor found some merit in the idea that if GCSE subjects outside the national curriculum took 10 per cent of the time, they could be trimmed a little and given 7.5 per cent. Another suggestion was to give the extended core plus history and geography 70 per cent of the time and let art and music fight it out with the rest of the subjects, which is what very largely happened.

The 70/30 proposal would have given everybody what they wanted if the various interest groups had not by that time been determined to fight each individual battle. The proposal was, however, bound to be attacked by the independent schools which were into the argument about the three sciences and the classics. Both they and ministers were losing sight of what was happening in the majority of the country's schools.

A 1988 study showed that at GCSE only about 80 per cent of children were studying English and maths, 30 per cent a modern language, and 30 per cent either history or geography. Overwhelmingly, girls were doing home economics and boys were doing technical subjects, and hardly any were doing art or PE. There was nothing that could be remotely called a balanced curriculum at 14, never mind pre-A-levels at 16.

MacGregor thought NCC had found a good solution but he did warn me that the pressures to drop subjects would continue. In keeping his options open, he wrote:

I would now like your council to think a little more widely about the possibilities at key stage 4, not ruling out the possibility that some subjects might be dropped by more pupils than I had envisaged in my speech.

He specifically asked the council to consider art, music and physical education as they were subjects in which most pupils would not be taking GCSE. They would not be given much lesson time and there was scope for them outside the formal curriculum.

The council still had to make up its mind which of the proposals it favoured but I told MacGregor it was worth him looking at what was being discussed, that the council would be open to further suggestions, and that it would discuss all the proposals at its annual residential conference. At last the council had the debate which until then it had signally failed to obtain.

The entire NCC, including David Pascall, who had just been appointed to it by MacGregor, subscribed to the very clear position that it was not going to have subjects dropped. I put the view to members that at the age of 15 it would be disastrous to compel children to do art and music but if they followed a course in, for example, performing arts, breadth and balance was secured. While clear in its own mind, the council said that other options would be put out to consultation. In the consultation, most people, including industry and commerce, were in favour of the 70/30 solution. Only the independent schools were against it. The consultation, which was published in November, was overwhelmingly in favour of a solution that although it might trim subjects would not drop them, to the chagrin of both the civil servants and HMI who were insinuating that NCC had pushed the national curriculum too far.

The consultation report went to MacGregor with a strong recommendation that NCC's proposal should be adopted. It did give him most of what he wanted. He was happy with history and geography. With art and music reduced he had found room for what he wanted. Then Mrs Thatcher moved him out of the Education Department in the wake of Sir Geoffrey Howe's resignation.

Within a few days of MacGregor's departure, Kenneth Clarke, the new Secretary of State, came to York for the official opening of NCC headquarters in November. We met in my room at three in the afternoon when the ceremony was over to discuss a number of things, but primarily key stage 4. Peter Watkins and I put forward NCC's proposals. Members of the council had done the same and had buttonholed him during the opening because there had been rumours from the Education Department that the new Secretary of State was not happy with the council's proposals. Clarke listened, asked questions, and said he could not see any particular flaws in the argument. But I knew from his face that he was not going to have it. The decision would have little to do with logic. He gave his initial views on key stage 4 a few days later in an interview in *The Times*, the first he had given since his appointment, when he said: 'It is not instantly apparent that they [NCC] have taken in what has been said. The curriculum must not become prescriptive and exclude the whole variety of options that people want to exercise.'

NCC did not hear from him again until he spoke to the North of England Education Conference in January. I only knew what he was going to say the night before he said it when he rang to tell me. The gesture was no more than a cold courtesy. I remember telling him with all the power at my command that the council had given advice of a very clear nature which had overwhelming support. I pointed out to him that night that it was going to be extremely embarrassing for NCC, who had not heard from him since the first week in November despite requests to meet him before important decisions were made. The council was told that he was too busy, that he was angry with it for having made a complete mess of key stage 4, that he was not going to have it, and that the council was trying to force through its own views of a national curriculum that people did not want.

I realised then that if a Secretary of State was prepared to treat a well-disposed advisory council in that way he would be prepared to do anything if it suited him. At the North of England Conference a year after MacGregor had raised the question of key stage 4, Clarke rejected the advice of NCC. Children would be required to take only mathematics, science, and English at GCSE. All pupils from the age of 11 to 16 would also have to take courses in a modern language and technology, but not necessarily to GCSE. At 14, children would have to take either history or geography or a course combining both. Music and art would be optional but all children would be expected to take some sort of physical exercise which could range from organised sport to aerobics.

Rejecting the council's advice, Clarke said:

> I believe we should not impose a rigid curriculum that leaves little scope for choice. By 14, young people are beginning to look at what lies beyond compulsory schooling, whether in work or further study. We must harness that sense of anticipation if every pupil is to have the chance of developing to the full.

I remain unconvinced. A 70/30 split offering breadth and balance did not seem unreasonable given the need in England to ensure that the pre-1988 state of affairs was not perpetuated.

All the evidence must be that had the problem of key stage 4 been tackled earlier we would have avoided much of the confusion and argument and found a better solution. There would certainly have been more time for a rational discussion of the council's final proposals, which the more I look at them the more they seem perfectly valid and sensible.

Following MacGregor's departure there was much discussion about what he would have done had he stayed at the Education Department. I can only say that he left me with the impression that in the light of the evidence of support he was more likely to come down bravely on the side of NCC although he would probably have made some changes, if only to show who was Secretary of State. The civil servants, not surprisingly, conveyed the message that he would not have accepted it. I personally wonder about that. If he rejected the advice it would only have been because of the overwhelming pressure on him. I can only say that on the whole MacGregor thought the solution was right, rather admired it, and would have liked to have accepted it.

9

NCC BEGINS TO CRUMBLE

The biggest single frustration of the National Curriculum Council was its inability to carry out the monitoring and evaluation of the curriculum after its introduction to schools as Kenneth Baker had promised on my appointment. One of my concerns then was whether the council would have a continuing role or be disbanded once the curriculum had been introduced. Baker's response was quite explicit. Had it not been, I doubt whether I would have accepted the post. He said the council had been set up by statute and it would require another to disband it. He said the council would move on from the role of implementation to the role of monitoring and evaluation. When Baker went it became clear that this was not going to be the case.

The importance of this question far transcends the rise or fall of the National Curriculum Council. The national curriculum machinery in England is of unparalleled complexity and largely untried. In order to make sure that the national curriculum develops as it should, delivers higher standards, has greater relevance, and does not present undue difficulties to schools and pupils, it will have to be regularly reviewed, from the nuts and bolts to the overall strategy. The right compromise will have to be struck between the need for change and the desire to leave things be when schools are coping with them.

Most national curriculums tend to ossify as time is not found for revising legislation, and as a result tablets of stone emerge. There is an absolute need for a body with expertise and independence to ensure that any change is soundly based and not subject to political whim or prejudice. It is reasonable to see this task as the main role for NCC in the future. If it is not to be, as was envisaged at the outset, then the question arises as to government's good intentions. The decline of Her Majesty's Inspectors of schools heightens one's suspicions and unease.

On succeeding Baker as Secretary of State for Education, John MacGregor told the council that the budget should be reduced now that

there were fewer subjects to be worked on and the council's res-
ponsibilities were winding down. I told him that this could not be, that it
was a betrayal of all that I had been led to believe was the council's
birthright. It must be allowed to evaluate the day-by-day working of the
curriculum and to answer fundamental questions: did people understand
it? Was it misleading people? Was it being applied fairly across the
country? The budget required might be less, it might be more. Expenditure of less than £10 million a year for servicing a national curriculum
could hardly be described as generous. My words had no effect, and the
message from MacGregor was clear and became clearer under Kenneth
Clarke, who succeeded him. NCC would have to cut back on its
programmes and staff rather than extend them. In the last year I was there
the council was told that no further permanent staff were to be appointed.

While the council was introducing the curriculum it was not too
worried about research into the effects, but once it had been successfully
implemented members believed it was essential that they should see how
it was working and how it could be improved. HMI, however, insisted
that this was their job: they would inspect schools, they would tell
ministers and the council how the national curriculum was working and
how it should be improved. This may well have been as a result of
growing insecurity. It is clear that HMI could not inspect and report on a
curriculum objectively if in due course it contained changes made at their
instigation. The council took the opposing view: unless it did some monitoring and evaluation of its own, based on independent evidence, it
would be powerless to recommend the changes that would inevitably be
necessary. Its first request to carry out such research went to Angela
Rumbold, the Minister of State. Mrs Rumbold was right to be suspicious
that the council was being over-ambitious and she was right to worry that
it might fall into the clutches of the researchers, but we did come to an
agreement and the first modest research began. When Rumbold was
replaced by Tim Eggar it became clear that he had no intention of allowing
the council to carry out any meaningful research into the application of
the curriculum. Eggar's approach to monitoring laid down the government's general approach to the council's budget as a means of control.

Out of the total budget of between nine and ten million a proportion
would be earmarked as expenditure for a number of items which might
include monitoring and evaluation. The money would only be released once
its detailed expenditure had been agreed. In effect, the government gave the
money with one hand, took away an increasing amount with the other, and
invited the council to come back and bid for it. Everything to do with
monitoring and evaluation had to be specifically approved by a minister and
funded by money that had already been earmarked for the purpose. In
practice, the council had no independent means of researching in any area a
minister might find uncongenial – a potentially worrying situation.

The question of NCC's relationship with HMI was brought to a head with its submission to Eggar. He quite properly said that until there was absolute clarity about the roles of HMI and NCC, the government was not going to fund two groups to do the same thing.

It is fair to say that our initial submissions for monitoring and evaluation were not as good as they could have been. The problem was the gulf between the proper professional aspirations of the staff and the political reality. The council's staff had still not learned that asking ministers for money for research was a very difficult thing to do and that the case had to be argued as never before. Some senior staff, even at deputy level, had memories of winning money in the halcyon days when budgets were open-ended and time-scales leisurely.

The first submission, part-written by Chris Woodhead who later became chief executive of NCC, was well-intentioned but lacked the rhetoric of rigour and all the key words that might have found favour, and also failed to set targets to raise standards. So in September 1990 Eggar turned NCC down flat. Monitoring was to be limited to reading, writing and arithmetic and therefore any original research was quite un-neccessary. The council should rely on HMI to provide the information it required. Any attempt to address the broader questions of the core subjects in context was precluded.

The council's position was that although much information could be provided by HMI, it did need access to a front-line monitoring and evaluation team. Perhaps driven by a fundamental fear that the council might end up proving that the national curriculum was not working, or worse still not cost-effective, and reveal things they did not want to know, ministers continued to turn down any proposals from it. (So much of recent change has not been scrutinised or piloted that it is quite likely that flaws would be revealed and changes required.) The council went back twice to Eggar and increasingly found itself being thrust into the most mechanistic system of evaluation imaginable, losing any pretence of being what the education service could be entitled to expect from a national body.

The only argument advanced by ministers that had any real validity was that if NCC pinpointed too many difficulties and chopped and changed too many things, teachers, parents and pupils would be confused. The answer to that is consultation with schools and parents and a bit of clear agreed planning. Fear of the results of monitoring and evaluating is always a worrying sign. The council defended its position on the grounds that HMI had their own agenda, used time-honoured and effective anecdotal methods of reporting which were not suitable for detailed scientific analysis and in any event could not guarantee to give the council everything that was required. The council could not, for example, order an in-depth look at primary school mathematics at levels 2 and 3. All it could do was to ask HMI if, during the course of its normal work, they could look at primary mathematics and provide any information they found useful but not conclusive.

NCC was unanimous in saying that it would use HMI, but would also want to know more and more from local education authorities, carry out some very limited front-line work of its own, and commission some additional research. That was where the fundamental battle line was drawn and for me personally it was make or break. It was not an empire building exercise. The council never contemplated employing any class-room researchers of its own, but a politically inspired curriculum had to be objectively evaluated. This was and is the *sine qua non*.

I referred ministers and officials back to the talk with Baker on my very first day, in which he agreed that unless NCC was able to undertake fundamental monitoring to enable it to give advice on how to upgrade and update the national curriculum as its remit specifically required, it did not really have a reason for existence once the curriculum had been introduced. One can argue that situations change, but I saw that battle as the one that decided whether or not I stayed with NCC, whether it had a real future and, therefore, if any kind of independent curriculum view as distinct from a political view had a future.

Progress here was also the only way that NCC could keep its highly talented staff and attract any future staff, as good-quality people would not be content with merely producing non-statutory guidance and then disappearing into the night. There were the most terrible morale problems. There was a professional staff of no more than 20 and it is remarkable how much they achieved in what became a very difficult atmosphere. If they were going to do the deep, detailed work of introducing subjects and rewriting non-statutory guidance, the only thing that would keep them going was a feeling that within their own subject areas and across the curriculum they would be able to find out what was happening on the ground in a programme of pragmatic research which would directly help schools to deliver the curriculum in such a way that standards would rise and with the most effective use being made of teachers' time and energy.

The future of the National Curriculum Council hung in the balance for the first time at Betwys-y-Coed. It hung for the second time on the whole question of monitoring, which was thrashed out in a series of meetings in the autumn of 1990 during MacGregor's time with Eggar and later became entangled with Clarke. MacGregor took no overt part in this at first, having delegated the problem to Eggar.

As I had turned for help to David Hancock in Baker's time, so I turned to John Caines his successor as permanent secretary. I told him that monitoring and evaluation was not just a minor issue but was fundamental to the future of NCC. I pointed out that his officials had been saying the council would have to lose staff once the implementation was over, which would of course rule out any monitoring. The running down of the council was perfectly valid if that was the government's policy but the position should be made clear. Was my job now to wind down the body I had just established? Caines was non-committal but repeated that the council should persist in trying to find an accommodation with HMI. He suggested that I spoke again to Eric Bolton, the Senior Chief HMI. For the first time it occurred to me that HMI itself might also be under threat and that they might have come to realise that the council was more likely to be an ally than an opponent.

The council came to a concordance with HMI which was a very sensible one – what a pity it could not have come earlier. HMI accepted that it could not guarantee to do all the research that we wanted on the time-scale the council required because they had their own imperatives. HMI would monitor the national curriculum as they did other aspects of education, but they could not recommend specific changes to it; the convention was confirmed that no body could inspect the working through of its own recommendations. The council would tell HMI what its programme was, ask what aspects of it they could undertake, and then commission the rest. HMI could draw NCC's attention to areas where they were consistently finding problems, but the council would have to find the solutions. It would be NCC's duty to advise the Secretary of State on specific changes to the national curriculum. He could then ask HMI for their observations on these proposals which would be quite legitimate, better informing him on the likely outcomes of recommended changes. This was a very sensible arrangement and created a proper and continuing role for the National Curriculum Council while confirming HMI in their role. NCC and HMI resolved all the outstanding problems and the animosity was properly resolved. As it happens it was one of the last things that Eric Bolton, whose personal contribution to the national curriculum was considerable, did before he retired and Clarke emasculated the inspectorate.

In the end such money as there was for evaluation was in my view sufficient to keep the door open, although in fact there has been little genuine monitoring. Ministers after Baker had always been opposed to it but the antagonism grew when Eggar was joined by the junior minister Michael Fallon who believed that NCC was dangerously left wing. On the plus side the relationship with HMI was sorted out and the staff could move some reasonable way forward, but I have to say that I felt let down. What was required was a generous recognition of the need to make progress in an atmosphere of trust and with a clear agenda.

A proper evaluation and monitoring system would have been invaluable when it came to reviewing the mathematics and science attainment targets in order to make them more suitable for testing with the GCSE. The examining boards, SEAC, and some heads (notably from independent schools) had persuaded the government to seek a reduction in the attainment targets, particularly in key stage 4.

David Pascall, who succeeded me as chairman, announced in October 1991 that the National Curriculum Council had agreed to reduce the key stage 4 targets from seventeen to four in science, one fewer than that suggested by the government, and from fourteen to five in mathematics as proposed by the government. Pascall described it as fine tuning. The arguments preceding the decision were far from fine and nobody was in tune. The original proposals were made before anybody had fully realised the implications for schools when all the national curriculum subjects were in place. As the council worked through the other subjects it began to recommend fewer attainment targets with two or three becoming the norm, both to avoid complexity and also to combine aspects of knowledge and understanding to meet the government's demands for practical attainment targets. Towards the end of the MacGregor era and the beginning of Clarke's, it became clear that there were very good arguments for revising the attainment targets in mathematics and science to free up the curriculum, reduce the burden on teachers, and to make them more compatible with GCSE.

The argument against change was – apart from this being a very nasty case of examinations driving the curriculum – that the national curriculum had hardly got off the ground, and that the changes were going to be made without the slightest evidence of how the mathematics and science curriculums had been working in schools. The changes were likely to confuse and annoy teachers who had already made detailed lesson plans. The argument against immediate review was supported by the insistence of ministers that nothing should be done to reduce the rigour or content of the courses. MacGregor also had to reassure Mrs Thatcher who had let it be known that any suggestion that mathematics and science were being downgraded would not be politically acceptable. Not for the first time, NCC was faced with the paradox of the government talking about a return to basics and the need to avoid over-complexity and over-prescription while at the same time being determined not to see mathematics and science reduced. Any changes would have to reduce the complexity but could not reduce the content.

My own view was that on balance it would be better to wait and not to pre-empt change in the light of experience, but it was decided to go ahead with the review. The question immediately arose as to who was to undertake the revision which became part of the argument over the future role of the council in reviewing the national curriculum. I assumed that here at last was what the National Curriculum Council had been set up for. The review may have been premature but NCC was the only body properly equipped to carry it out, consulting widely and with assistance from all of those who were interested. It would have been an open exercise, with the views of teachers and parents being heard.

Without being consulted I then heard, as against being told, that the review was to be carried out by HMI and that NCC would carry out the consultation on the proposals. The decision, which was made by Kenneth Clarke who had replaced MacGregor, seemed to conflict with the convention that HMI should not recommend changes which they would later be asked to judge. HMI were certainly aware of the difficulty. Strangely, the argument, when I protested violently, was that the council could not propose changes and then consult on them. I could not see how the council could possibly be compromised by consulting on proposals it had made after hearing all the evidence. It is common practice elsewhere in government.

By then NCC was being blamed for the over-complexity of the curriculum and being accused of empire building, and ministers were simply determined that whatever happened it was not going to be allowed to undertake the review. From that moment on it was obvious that the council was not going to be allowed to review the curriculum at all because whatever recommendations it made in the future would have to go out to consultation and it could not, therefore, make the original recommendations. Ironically, the mathematics and science inspectors were reluctant to take on the task because they, too, believed the review was premature but HMI were in no position to refuse as Clarke was beginning to question their own role. Council members were much perturbed at being kept out and I finally obtained agreement to involve NCC's professional officers, who were far better prepared to do the job than HMI as they had lived and breathed the mathematics and science orders for three years and knew all the technicalities. When the final recommendations were made it was impossible to divine the individual contributions from NCC staff or HMI.

The restrictions on research and review were the major elements of determined attempts to restrict the activities of NCC but they were not the only ones. Ministers, particularly Eggar and Fallon, saw every initiative as dangerous. In spite of evidence to the contrary, NCC was seen as being in the hands of the professionals, the educationists and the teachers. Certainly these two ministers moved in every direction to curtail the activities of the council, particularly in the publication of documents. It was not possible to fulfil their agenda with any sense of impartiality or independence. From the beginning it was decided that everything that NCC published had to be approved by the Secretary of State. The council readily accepted that statutory and formal documents could only be prudently published with the full knowledge and approval of the Secretary of State. There was also the pragmatic argument that the council would be foolish to publish a major paper with which the Secretary of State was unhappy. This was not to say that the council should only publish what was approved but that there could be sensible discussion and acceptable compromise before publication. There were other areas where according to its remit NCC should be free to publish as it thought fit. I believe that the paper on the whole curriculum and the five non-statutory documents on the cross-curricular themes of citizenship, health, industrial and economic understanding, the environment and careers fell into this area.

The council believed it had a responsibility to help teachers by producing useful guidance in order to humanise the curriculum by getting away from the dead hand of statutory language, but found that its ability to do so was severely limited. It soon discovered that all of this was subject to word-by-word approval, by civil servants if not ministers. The case put by officials was that they were acting on behalf of ministers to spot any potential difficulties that the council had missed, although they rarely came up with any real criticism. The council was told it could only publish documents which fell very narrowly within its remit, anything else had to be left to the Education Department. That meant NCC could not say a word about teaching methods and resources or publish anything directly for parents unless it was asked to do so.

Competition between NCC, the Education Department, HMI, and later SEAC, led to a proliferation of publications and a plethora of newsletters and various DES updates. Using its considerable budget, the DES then embarked on a vast range of documents, some of which were actively alienating because of their tone and style. Perhaps predictably, HMI was moved to defend its independence with a spate of publications, most of which were strictly irrelevant. Once the national curriculum was in place the majority of HMI documents, no matter how good or interesting to the education historian, were of less immediate value to schools or teachers and could be misleading and distracting. Teachers on the whole, particularly in primary schools, were not sure of the status of each document and tended to attach more importance to those from HMI even if they were out-of-date.

In all of this there were two sustainable arguments. One was to argue that no matter how many publications there were, there was a case for all of them provided that schools were given guidance as to how they should regard them. The other was either that publication was phased in such a way as to make for coherence or that some central judgement should be made as to what was published. It was the council's view from the start that common sense arrangements should be made to control the flow and give guidance on the priority of documents. Because of all the vested interests which were involved the flood continued and the schools started to react against the piles of documents arriving every day. I remember one headmaster describing it as death by a thousand ring binders – and he had a point.

My objective judgement, as far as it can be, is that much, although not all, of what NCC put out was necessary – certainly very little was not sold out or reprinted. If there was too much it was because the pace of change was too great, not because the material was unnecessary. It would not have mattered much to the council if other agencies had produced some of its documents. It was the lack of planning which was so frustrating for NCC and, ultimately, for ministers.

During this period MacGregor and his ministers began to express concern at the complaints they were receiving from schools about the number of documents being sent to them. Angela Rumbold was charged with the task of investigating how this should be brought under control. She called a meeting at which the DES, HMI, NCC and SEAC were all present. She had obviously been briefed by her officials and at that point she was rather tending to take the view that the DES publications were pre-eminent and that the rest were subservient. Mrs Rumbold asked if we would all agree to a corporate timetable which would ensure that no more than two documents went out in any one month and that by charting ahead we could avoid an avalanche of paper hitting schools. She also asked that we all observe a voluntary self-denying ordinance that would mean that we would not publish anything that was not essential. The shock of seeing all the documents piled in front of us was quite a salutory experience for all of us and with one exception we all agreed to cut back.

HMI indicated that they would not be bound by the agreement and could not be bound by it as their independence required them to publish as they saw fit, but for the rest of us the system worked quite well. HMI, on the other hand, appeared to publish even more, if only because they had more on the stocks. Regular and reasonably amicable meetings with Mrs Rumbold followed, the arrangement over publications worked quite well, and we managed to agree what we would and would not do. The number of complaints from schools was reduced, although they were not removed entirely.

The atmosphere changed when Rumbold was replaced by Eggar. He became much more militant about reducing the number of documents. His only evidence seemed to be that overburdened heads were continually telling him that they were receiving far too much. There was an element of truth in this but of course when people are asked if there is a problem they inevitably say that there is. Eggar, who could often appear to be a bully, chose to believe that everything that went to a school was for the head and he could not accept the argument that certain documents were intended for the heads of various departments within a school. If you sent a careers document, for example, then it was intended for the careers teacher.

Not long after his appointment Eggar called a meeting, which was also attended by Michael Fallon, to discuss the situation. It was the first of a series of difficult meetings where both men were unpleasantly and calculatingly critical not only of the quantity of documents but of their quality.

It emerged that ministers were not particularly interested in the views of the professionals. At one point Fallon picked up a SEAC newsletter and said that it was the biggest waste of the taxpayers' money he had ever seen. No sane person, never mind a teacher, would read such rubbish. He then gave similar treatment to a NCC newsletter. It is true that the news-letters were not riveting reading but they were vitally important in telling people the mundane but important things they had to know about the timetable of the curriculum, examinations and testing. The requirements were statutory and obligatory. Eggar then ruled that only DES statutory guidance, NCC non-statutory guidance, and formal examination guid-ance from SEAC could go directly to schools. Even the officials were under fire: having created the problem they then found themselves the victims of the solution. In effect, nothing could go out without specific ministerial approval and all the council could do was to let people know which documents were available and invite them to order them by post. The market forces argument was that if people wanted NCC publications they would ask for them. This did, however, create the quite remarkable situation that although teachers were bound by a statutory national curriculum the body responsible for it was no longer allowed to tell them everything they ought to know about how to implement it.

The inevitable happened, of course. Good schools continued to ask for practically everything, others did not and we were back to the inequalities that the national curriculum was designed to reduce. Meanwhile, the paradox continued. There was little slackening off in the complaints about too much information coupled with a huge demand for everything that was produced.

The second unfortunate outcome of Eggar's publication pronouncement was, according to my calculations, an increase in costs, as from then on nobody knew how many copies to print of each document. There were the twin problems of the waste of over-printing and the delay in meeting orders when reprints had to be rearranged. The councils had to increase their clerical staffs to cope with requests for publications. Instead of sending ten copies of everything to every school the council had staff sitting in York waiting for orders of between 15,000 and 20,000 for each publication which could not be distributed across the country cost- effectively.

The council developed a subscription service where everything could be ordered with one letter every year. A considerable number of schools used the service but a considerable number did not. This may have been more of a commentary on the organisation of some schools rather than a statement on their real needs as the council then received letters from schools complaining that they had had not received certain documents it turned out that they had not asked for. The tone of correspondence to NCC turned from the odd letter saying that they were getting too much to an avalanche of complaints that documents were not being received.

The council's problems did not end once publication had been agreed in principle. Everything had to be improved and edited to meet the special interests of ministers and officials, not necessarily those in the Education Department. The five documents on the cross-curricular themes of citizenship, health, the environment, industrial and economic understanding and careers were the most obvious example of ministerial panic and interference. John MacGregor in particular had been impressed with the argument from the independent schools that they would undermine standards as they would deflect from the main curriculum. This was a complete misunderstanding of their purpose. Teachers would want to enter these areas and the booklets were intended to guide them in ways which enhance the curriculum not detract from it.

Once publication of the booklets was agreed it was open season for anybody with a particular point of view to seek to sell it. David Waddington, who was then the Home Secretary, was first into the field as NCC came to prepare the guidance on citizenship, but it was not very long before Donald Acheson, the then chief medical officer, was into sorting out NCC's guidance on health, having been alerted by the Home Office.

Citizenship was already a delicate political area as the government viewed the recently announced Speaker's Commission on Citizenship as being dangerously left wing. Waddington took the view that it was up to the council to tell teachers in every school what they should teach. Specifically, teachers should concentrate on the evils of car thefts and the need to co-operate with the police.

When I went to the Home Office to see David Waddington and John Patten, who was appointed Secretary of State for Education after the 1992 general election, John MacGregor was there and I was given a DES minder. The Home Office saw the citizenship booklet as a propaganda medium rather than an exercise in educating young people to participate and discriminate before making their own judgements. The official was very courageous, making it clear to Waddington in no uncertain terms that the guidance was educational and not part of a crime prevention campaign. The official must have known as we all did that at that time Waddington was closer to Margaret Thatcher than was MacGregor, the latter already being under considerable pressure from his right wing.

MacGregor became very concerned about what the citizenship document would say and as NCC had by then apparently won the battle for independence I showed him the draft to reassure him. He did not change anything, but I had before I sent it to him. The team who had written it had put rights before duties and I turned it round to duties before rights. Presentation is all!

The document on economic and industrial understanding was launched personally by John MacGregor, so we went full circle from outright obstruction to an endorsement from the Secretary of State. He was delighted with the booklet because it brought together education and the world of work, which he saw as crucial to the country's economic success.

The comings and goings over the right to publish show how the mixture of internecine strife and ministerial misinterpretation very often ended up in damaging the service to schools which did not always receive the documents they needed. When they did receive them they were often late. Ministerial intervention should not have been necessary but when it came it could have been better directed. The schools were the losers. Local authorities, heads and teachers wrote to ask the council how they could be expected to introduce the national curriculum if they could not even be sent a copy of the relevant document. If ministers sought to achieve a cheap victory over the alien bodies of NCC, SEAC, and to some extent the DES and HMI, they signally failed.

Few who embarked on the great adventure of the national curriculum thought other than that such a massive gamble would need to be watched, measured, adjusted, and revised. It seemed essential that the job should be done publicly with the views of all those involved taken into account. It had to be done objectively and professionally to avoid the political dangers inherent in a national curriculum. It is a matter of regret that the National Curriculum Council which was set up to carry out the task has not been allowed to do so. It is of much greater concern that the job is not being done at all. It is essential to the future well-being of the national curriculum that open independent review takes place. Ministers must come clean on this and re-establish trust and professional dialogue.

The National Curriculum Council itself would undoubtedly be in a stronger position had it not made the mistake of abandoning its committees of professionals who were there to offer advice to members and officers. A group of members felt that they no longer wanted to attend committees where they would be outnumbered by professionals. That was understandable, but it was always clear that final decisions lay with the council. It did highlight the problems facing a membership comprised of some with a wide professional knowledge and others who were laymen. Both have useful contributions to make, but both must see the other's point of view.

Kenneth Baker had warned that NCC would lose credibility if it ever became the mouthpiece of the Secretary of State for Education, the education profession, the unions, or any other group of professionals. He was quite happy for the council to have its views while he had his. It was sometimes difficult to maintain a detached view and occasionally in the first year some members of the staff found themselves talking for teachers, telling them that they would return to the council and fight their corner as distinct from saying that they would take account of their views along with those of all the others.

NCC did, with Baker's approval, work closely with the teacher unions and did sometimes ask them to suggest a number of suitable names to serve on committees. There were individual exceptions but the unions were allies in the sense that in time they began to tell their members that the national curriculum was, generally speaking, a good thing, that the council's heart was in the right place, and that they ought to work with it. They were very helpful in not opposing the national curriculum once the Education Reform Act had been passed.

The next logical step from the committees would have been to set up a more formal partnership with teachers and local education authorities to allow them to have a real say in the development of the national curriculum. I had always argued that it was all very well to impose a national curriculum on people and to insist that they did something in which they had not been professionally involved in order to galvanise them into action, but the essential concomitant was that there would be an eventual return to partnership.

Unless teachers take the national curriculum to be their own within a wider partnership and are given some kind of role in curriculum development, there will be no real progress in raising standards. The game plan, which nobody contested, was that once the short sharp shock had been delivered and the curriculum was beginning to enter schools, the council would reopen partnership with teachers and the local education authorities to give them more overt involvement in the national curriculum. That has not happened, even though it has been shown that where teachers have become involved, as they did in testing, for example, there have been improvements.

I believed NCC should have set up a regional network with the authorities, their education officers and advisory staff who, after all, are the people who have to implement the national curriculum. Every conceivable obstacle was put in the council's way because of the unremitting hostility to local education authorities from all ministers, including Baker. The council argued that while the authorities remained it should have dealings with them. Ministers chose to pretend that the authorities did not exist and as a result the council was not permitted to have a formal relationship with them. The council should also have had a good relationship with colleges and departments of education. The national curriculum could not possibly be introduced without having some influence on teacher training but the council soon discovered that training was one of the many things it was not supposed to touch.

Had NCC liaised with the colleges and the local authorities it might have forestalled the argument over traditional and progressive teaching methods which marked Kenneth Clarke's last few months in office. It was quite obvious that primary school teachers were ill-equipped to teach the nine-subject national curriculum and that teaching methods relying on topic work were not suitable in the majority of schools.

The National Curriculum Council set out to be a key player in a network of partnerships in which it did not see itself in any sense as god-like or authoritarian but certainly as having a statutory place. A network would have been a very effective way of getting over all the reforms and would have allowed the council to work more closely with schools. Prejudice from ministers, rivalry between the various interest groups involved in the national curriculum and, finally, divisions within NCC itself, meant that the opportunity was lost.

10

THE TIME TO LEAVE

When Kenneth Clarke was appointed as Secretary of State for Education it seemed that his first major policy decision was to throw out everything that was waiting in his in-tray and to start again. As far as the National Curriculum Council was concerned the biggest casualty was of course key stage 4 and, in a sense, the council itself.

How much of his pugnacity was caused by the fact that he had not wanted to leave the Department of Health is difficult to judge. He certainly had not expected to be moved in the mini-shuffle caused by the resignation of Sir Geoffrey Howe and said publicly that he was amazed when Mrs Thatcher announced her plans. He told *The Times*: 'I told my staff [in the Department of Health] the night before that the two cabinet ministers who would not be moved, because of the reforms going through, were John MacGregor and me.'

Once in the Education Department he seemed determined to distance himself as much as he could from MacGregor – indeed from everything that had gone before. By then, there was a whispering campaign against Kenneth Baker who was being blamed at the very least for appointing people who were determined to wreck the government's education reforms through the national curriculum. Right-wing Conservatives were labelling the curriculum as too complex and over-prescriptive, which was fair but the fault of the government, and too soft and liberal, which it certainly was not.

Whatever the reasons, Clarke came to the Education Department prejudiced against the National Curriculum Council and the School Examinations and Assessment Council, viewing them rather quaintly as creations of an opposition government, certainly not his own. Education Department officials, to their credit, fought manfully to ensure fair play. From the moment Baker went, and not because MacGregor himself was hostile but because ministers no longer felt a sense of ownership, NCC and SEAC came under increasing pressure.

The blame for the problems faced by schools in delivering the national curriculum and its attendant tests was to be pinned on the two councils which now had no more status than any other pressure groups, perhaps less. There is no question of this being a personal prejudice against the members of NCC and SEAC but a deep-seated distrust of any advice from professionals whose judgement Clarke believed would be tarnished by their own prejudices. He seemed to believe that the government had been forced into a strait-jacket and it was being left to him to untie the straps. As in the past, the situation was worsened by the tensions that often seemed to exist betwen ministers within the same department. Each had his or her own agenda and there was little evidence to suggest that matters were discussed with colleagues before statements were issued or decisions taken. The depth of division varied as individual politicians came and went while the civil servants stayed.

Relations between Baker and Angela Rumbold, his Minister of State, appeared to be distant, perhaps because while they were working together Rumbold was closer to Mrs Thatcher than he was. This special relationship did not appear to concern MacGregor who gave Rumbold more freedom. MacGregor acknowledged that Rumbold knew more about state education from her days as a councillor than he did and they got on quite well.

Any sense of isolation MacGregor may have felt must have increased with the appointment of Tim Eggar as Minister of State and Michael Fallon as the junior schools minister. I have a suspicion that from very early on MacGregor was being closely watched and that Eggar and Fallon had been drafted in as minders. From the moment they arrived there was a noticeable feeling of discord between him and the two junior ministers. It was never overt but it was always there. Eggar seemed to be there for personal advancement, Fallon as the direct representative of the right wing.

The feeling grew progressively through MacGregor's period in office that all was not well with the three men. Eggar and Fallon were watching MacGregor while he was looking over his shoulder at them. Eggar acted almost independently of MacGregor in some fields. I went to see Eggar at the House of Commons to discuss a range of issues shortly after he was appointed in August 1990. Having had a good relationship with Baker and Rumbold, to whom I also had access, I thought there ought to be a similar arrangement with Eggar.

The first meeting with Eggar was extremely difficult. He was visibly prejudiced against the council and what it was doing. He was full of talk about the over-production of documents and moved into the first attack in what was, in a sense, to lead to the downfall of the National Curriculum Council: that the over-complexity of the national curriculum was deliberate and that the blame lay with NCC. I can think of nothing more unfair. NCC did not invent – and would not have invented – the national curriculum as laid down in the 1988 Education Reform Act which also created NCC.

Eggar asked: why, over the last two years, had the council not taken steps to simplify the curriculum? Why had it been allowed to become even more complicated? And why had the council not sorted out the way teachers taught? The hostility faded when we began to talk about the council's core skills document which he acknowledged helped to bridge the academic divide. We had a constructive discussion as he could see the possibility of moving into vocational education, which he eventually did. Eggar had a very good vision of 14 to 19 education. He could grasp that if education at 14 could be a mixture of academic and vocational it would be possible to lead young people on to sensible choices at 16. He was also willing to contemplate the fact that A-levels were not entirely ideal, while MacGregor was not.

It was agreed that I would see Eggar once every two months or so but I had to be careful that this did not become a substitute for seeing MacGregor, who had earlier agreed that we could meet if there was something I wanted to talk to him about. Discussions with MacGregor became more difficult, as when I did see him he would always have had a report from Eggar as well as papers from the civil servants and HMI. Fallon also intervened although he had little to do with the curriculum. He none the less kept turning up at meetings with MacGregor where he was overtly hostile. Natural courtesy was not Fallon's strong point. We once met on a train from York and he was not even prepared to exchange the time of day. I do not think his antagonism was personal, just a right-wing fear and dislike of professionals.

MacGregor was invariably easy to deal with and we had only one serious disagreement throughout our time together. I had given a speech to the annual conference of the Secondary Heads Association about the progress of the national curriculum which some newspaper reports had interpreted as an attack on government policy, which it was not. MacGregor had come to hear of it and became very angry, ringing me on NCC's car telephone during my return to York. He was uncharacteristically brisk. I let him finish and said that the speech had been misinterpreted and that I would send him a copy. Having read it, he was suitably apologetic but the incident did illustrate the pressure he was under. When he left education he wrote saying how much he appreciated our working relationship.

If things had been hard all along, the really difficult times started with the arrival of Clarke. Education secretaries are either on the way down or on the way up. Mrs Thatcher was the only one to become prime minister athough Baker believed for a while that he would replace her. MacGregor had no obvious ambitions but Clarke must have believed he had been given the job because he was on the way down. Once Mrs Thatcher had left Downing Street, Clarke seemed to see his chance of being reborn and it could be argued that he used his time in education to prove his right-wing credentials. In doing so he disturbed the peace that officials believed would settle over the DES with the departure of Mrs Thatcher.

The talk amongst officials was of relief that at last the single-minded relentless pressure on education would be off and that there would be no further lurches to the right. As it transpired, John Major, perhaps because of his own mixed experience of education, was anxious to become involved, and the combination of the prime minister and Clarke moved the emphasis very much to the right. As Clarke moved to the right, so Eggar moved with him. Fallon was able to stay where he was. The atmosphere around the Education Department also became very much more fraught. The influence of Major was part of that movement.

Ministers were straight into the attack over complexity and over-prescription, which became the new battle cry. The fact that the National Curriculum Council had been telling the government much the same for the previous two years did not prevent Clarke and his junior ministers heaping all the perceived or real ills of state education onto NCC and SEAC. Overnight, the people who had been praised by previous ministers for doing a good job had turned into those who had created the chaos of over-complexity in both curriculum and tests. Fallon, for example, would tell anybody who cared to listen that it was time for the National Curriculum Council to stop. Both he and Eggar were strident in their belief that the task of the council was to introduce the national curriculum and once that had been done the task was finished and it had no function. If the initial proposal had been to set up a body to introduce the national curriculum then one could argue that after five years it should go, but the government, through Baker, had not set up that kind of body. I was not employed to head such a body nor were the staff employed to work for it.

While being aware of the growing misgivings of ministers, I was never called in for a rational discussion. Ministers were not, as MacGregor had been, willing to consider adding to or updating the remit of the council. They were not keen to be reminded of the nature of the council as explained to me on my appointment by Baker. He told me shortly after my appointment that ministers had insisted on a National Curriculum Council because they realised that they would need totally independent professional advice over and beyond the kind they would get from the civil servants. Teachers would also need a source of independent educational advice and it would be better if schools were given that advice by people they saw as professionally credible. The National Curriculum Council was to fulfil both roles. Baker made it clear that he would expect its views to be complementary to but different from those of the civil servants. Baker recognised that he needed to keep these two sets of advice apart. Direct involvement in curriculum matters made it necessary to have more than generalist advice.

Both Baker and Rumbold believed there were dangers in the national curriculum if it passed into the hands of an unscrupulous minister and that the existence of NCC with a strong professional view would be a bulwark. The ultimate danger would be if the council itself became tied to politicians. Baker's views were in contrast to Clarke's. Baker wanted independent professional advice of high integrity and he certainly made it plain that he was not afraid of it. Clarke refused at times even to listen to that advice.

As the atmosphere worsened, difficulties also appeared within the council, with members angry that they were being both attacked and ignored by the new Secretary of State. He did agree to having dinner with the council in London in February but it was a difficult occasion. The members were very quiet and did not air their grievances. It became clear then that the future of NCC was in doubt.

While discontent with Clarke continued, some members saw me as a source of discontent and thought I was out of sympathy with the Secretary of State, which they believed led to him being unsympathetic to NCC, although this was never my impression when talking to Clarke. Members also believed that they were not being allowed to take their own decisions, that I and the staff were making all the running. The pace of change was such that this was to an extent inevitable. When members were given the opportunity for real debate, some of them had not done their homework. None the less they had a point. Whether the timetable could have been met had they been given their full say is a matter for debate.

This is the dilemma. Delivery or ridicule faced NCC and SEAC at every turn. Perhaps the staff suffered even more. They were given little time to settle in and adjust before having to produce detailed reports and proposals in the full glare of publicity.

As the discontent grew within NCC, ministers and some members began to question whether it was right to continue to combine the role of chairman and chief executive. When the appointment was made there had been good reasons for combining the two positions because of the magnitude of the task and the demands of the timetable. I was conscious then that these are always two difficult hats to wear. And so it proved. Staff tended to see me in a role beyond that of chief executive. Tensions always exist between officers and members, and while the staff largely sympathised they must at times have wished for firmer support from me than was possible. Council members were faced with the difficult task of analysing and criticising papers in which they knew their chairman had inevitably had a hand.

Conventions had to be set up for council meetings whereby the introduction and justification of documents were presented by members of the staff. When officers came under pressure, particularly if it was unfair, the temptation to defend them was strong but had to be resisted. In the early stages of the process when council members were finding their feet and detailed knowledge of what NCC was about was at a premium, the situation was bearable with goodwill all round. Later, as the members flexed their muscles and wished to assume more control over decisions, publications and the work of staff, the balancing act became progressively harder.

I had, of course, a separate relationship with ministers and DES officials from that of other NCC members and this too brought problems as ministers made extra demands and wanted to have a direct involvement in the curriculum. There were times when members clearly felt that I was taking too much upon myself, whilst I could have wished them to have had some deeper understanding of the problems and the pressures. In hindsight we could all no doubt have played it better but the reality was that combining the posts of chairman and chief executive was proving increasingly difficult. What made the situation even worse for me was a constant awareness of the impact of all that we did on schools and, above all, on pupils. It was not, as sometimes appeared, a rather arcane kind of game.

Council members had their own uncertainties about their role. Some felt that theirs was a watching brief to fine tune the work of officers in whom they had confidence. Others, while sharing the confidence in their officers, would have liked to exercise that detailed control which requires a lot of time and effort.

David Pascall, who had been appointed by MacGregor the previous summer, began to play a role. An oil executive who had once worked in Mrs Thatcher's policy unit at No. 10, he went on to become part-time chairman after my resignation when the posts of chairman and chief executive were split. On his arrival at the council, Pascall said that he believed the curriculum was far too complicated and that it would have to be simplified. He was openly critical of the way the council had been operating.

Between January and my departure I saw both Eggar and Clarke on a number of occasions, but they were seldom meetings of any substance and were overlaid by the knowledge that neither Eggar nor Clarke had much faith in NCC.

All of this combined to reinforce my first qualms about the job which had surfaced quite soon after I had repeated Baker's view of the council and its future role to the civil servants only to be greeted by a chilly silence. But from the spring of 1991, as I saw that NCC might have either a limited life or be hopelessly circumscribed, I knew that I did not want to be with it much longer. Those feelings were not based on personal ambition. I had achieved most of what I wanted in career terms but if I went on I wanted a worthwhile job.

Stories appeared in the newspapers that Clarke would abandon NCC and SEAC. My staff was clearly shaken by this but Clarke denied that this was in his mind and added that the rumour would keep the staff on their toes. I wish he had been able to see the effect the rumour had on decent hardworking people with families and mortgages. In fact the two chairmen and chief executives, myself at NCC and Philip Halsey at SEAC, left within a week of each other in July 1991 and there is renewed talk of combining the two councils sometime in the future.

In discussions with Clarke during the early summer of 1991 he and I honestly acknowledged that the circumstances that had brought about the dual role no longer prevailed and that the new situation was putting undue pressure upon NCC, its staff, and myself. I reminded him of my original intention on being appointed to stay for between three and five years. We moved towards the agreement that the time for change was coming, not least as the work of the council was moving from the introduction of the curriculum to a phase which, to put it mildly, I regarded as ill-defined. Our discussions were amicable but I decided that I no longer wanted to go on pretending that the National Curriculum Council was an important body credited with powers it clearly did not possess. I am quite happy to have had a hand in the introduction of the national curriculum but I could see other retreats on the horizon. Everywhere I went I was treated as if I and NCC had real powers to change things. The reality was different. In July 1991 I decided that the time had come for pastures new.

11

THE LESSONS OF CHANGE

The national curriculum – or, more accurately, a national curriculum – is here to stay. It is hard to envisage a political or even an educational reason for abandoning it. Surveys of parents, teachers, governors and local authorities have all indicated support ranging from the enthusiastic to the qualified. Most significantly, there are very few teachers who actively oppose the idea. The consensus is, however, superficial. When asked what changes or developments are desirable, unanimity disappears, reflecting the reservations and ambitions of different interests. This is no bad thing, as it will guarantee change and adaptation: the biggest threat to a national curriculum is that it becomes set in stone.

Now that it is more or less in place, it is possible to make a preliminary assessment of strengths and weaknesses leading on to potential change. It would be easier to do so had the government been courageous enough to encourage critical independent research into the effects of the curriculum and the way it is being handled in the classroom. At times it has seemed as if ministers feared the outcome of any research – perhaps standards are declining or it is less than cost effective when set against Treasury formulae. It may simply be an ingrained prejudice against research itself, and against those who carry it out.

Such monitoring as the National Curriculum Council was permitted to undertake, when taken together with reports from HMI, is encouraging if tentative. There is little evidence of active harm, although there is some concern about the demands of the curriculum in primary schools distracting teachers from concentrating on the basic skills, particularly reading. Against this, there are signs of some very positive progress, although it is too early to say whether the curriculum will justify the enthusiasm which so many of us felt at the beginning.

There are fears, too, that as so often happens when people take fright at change, that ministers will begin to nibble away at it, to reduce it to a shadow of what was originally intended to be broad and balanced. There is nothing broad and balanced about the three Rs. Let us hope that the present attempts of some of those involved in the introduction of the reforms to distance themselves from the curriculum is no more than that familiar panic most of us have in that period just after buying a new car before we get used to driving and servicing it.

When justifying the introduction of the curriculum, ministers were keen to point out that it was the decentralised nature of the English education system and its consequent patchiness which led to uneven standards and incompatible lessons. These local variations, it was said, inhibited the mobility of labour and made it difficult to define standards. The national curriculum was designed to provide the right kind of uniformity. The reformers could have used the word entitlement had it not been politically suspect. What happened in effect was that a government which passionately believed in market forces prescribed a curriculum for state schools in unparalleled detail. Whatever the battles behind the scenes about a narrow three Rs prescription, Kenneth Baker and his civil servants triumphed with a broad ten-subject curriculum. They were correct in terms of the scale of change needed, but it is little wonder that the right wing were soon trying to cancel the contract.

It is an open question as to the extent and scope of the curriculum that will finally emerge after a debate which will mirror the wider political arguments about how far a Conservative government should intervene rather than leaving everything to market forces. It is to be hoped that the apparently more flexible outlook of the 1992 Major government will find the right balance.

Few educational professionals would have gone for the awe-inspiring prescription set in train by the 1988 Education Reform Act but it was probably better to start at that end of the spectrum. It is easier to draw back, having made the required ritual noises about preserving rigour and depth, than to add. As with all master plans it is better to have something to depart from, rather than a blank sheet of paper.

There is evidence that the curriculum is now more balanced for more pupils than ever before. It is undoubtedly true that many primary pupils will again study history and geography and that science and technology will not depend upon accidents of teacher preference. Key stage 1 designed for 5- to 7-year-olds will improve the picture immeasurably. All schools will now have to do what good schools always did.

In secondary schools a modern language will be guaranteed at last, as will a balanced science which removes much of the gender-bias of the past and technology which will ensure more than a narrow craft design technology course for boys and home economics for girls. Within subjects, there can be little possibility of vital information and concepts being omitted. There is no longer scope for endless duplication and inadvertent overlap.

117

Eventual reform of the curriculum was inevitable the moment it was decided to introduce it subject by subject. The appointment of individual subject working groups guaranteed that zealots outnumbered cynics – always a dangerous thing – and that no subject would be knowingly undersold. When the full enormity of the consequences became clear, complexity and over-prescription became the cry of those who had caused it. Scapegoats were called for and found. None the less, if one had to err, it was a magnificent aberration. It remains true that while the scope and extent cause concern, there has been singularly little criticism of the content as such, and when the first attempts are made to cut it, there will be some splendid rows.

Embarrassing though it must appear to some on the right wing, every child now has an entitlement to a high-grade education whatever the school and wherever they live. The playing field has been levelled, and not just in the state sector. In time the disadvantaged, actual and potential, will reap the benefits. Equal opportunities exist in statutory form and in a manner which is only just beginning to be exploited in terms of demanding more resources. Governing bodies armed with a programme of study and a calculator can go far in defining their needs and making a good case for them to be met.

Although it is by nature harder to define, progress has been made in terms of breadth and balance and the whole curriculum. Few people would now dispute that there ought to be a framework which sets the aim and the purpose of eleven years of compulsory schooling. While it can be argued that themes, dimensions and skills have been submerged by parents and teachers in discussion about subject development, standard assessment tasks and the GCSE, and the wranglings about course-work and examinations, the evidence is that they have been influential in raising awareness and in shaping school curriculum plans.

While there is no room for complacency, the fear that only statutorily defined lessons would survive and be taught has so far proved to be unfounded: there is evidence of a more professional and systematic approach to planning and delivery of cross-curricular material, mirroring that of the formal curriculum. The traditional support for rationale, ethos and values which have epitomised the best of public and independent school practice, has been helpful. These schools demonstrate that with traditional subjects and the other things in life, there is room for both rather than the defeatist either/or – even if that does mean a longer school day.

There are other gains. The evidence is that curriculum planning and organisation are consistently to a higher standard than before – few primary pupils inadvertently receive a double-dose of the Vikings. There is a great deal to be done still in the difficult areas of progression and differentiation, but here, too, there are promising signs and a heightened awareness. The format of the national curriculum has helped, with detailed statements of attainment and examples of what and how things should be taught. These are far from perfect and deserve early revision by NCC and SEAC – but they do enable a clearer definition of individual achievement.

The possible move back towards whole-class teaching in some subjects will make it even more necessary to have strong guidance and material on differentiation – it is all too easy to teach to an average or assume too much. Ways of meeting the needs of the less able and the most able need to be properly examined and put into effect.

Provided that teachers and schools are given time to assimilate and absorb, provided that changes are minimised for the time being – and even desirable ones add to the confusion and the workload – the basic framework looks likely to raise standards across the country. We may in a sense be little closer to defining and providing the basics, but they are assuredly all there within the curriculum as it stands.

The freedom to decide how to teach is the professional birthright of the teacher, and teachers have on the whole been relieved to find that the careful attempts to distinguish between content and teaching methods, which are a feature of the Act, seem to have been successful. What has happened is a raising of awareness about the range of teaching methods which can be deployed and their relative strengths and weaknesses, so that schools are consciously examining which methods best serve which purpose and then significantly improving them rather than narrowing the choice. Where topic work is used, for example, particular care has to be taken to ensure that the statutory requirements are covered within it or systematically added. It appears that a balance is being more surely struck between the modern and more traditional methods. Attempts to use the national curriculum to support a return to streaming, or serried ranks of children in desks being taught by chalk and talk have so far failed.

The pressures to change teaching methods – a euphemism for a return to the formal approach – have not been inspired by the nature of the national curriculum. They originate in a tide of romantic traditionalism, a gut response to ministers' own school-days, and an over-reaction to anecdotal evidence of the perceived dangers of extreme teaching methods. No doubt some teachers could employ whole-class teaching more than they have done, but to see it as more than one important teaching technique is to go too far, to put prejudice before evidence. In no other area of life are hapless individuals subjected to instruction in mixed ability tranches of thirty or more.

It is to be hoped that the relative success of the curriculum is not offset by political interventions in methodology, based on the belief that it is possible to return to a fondly remembered and often illusory golden age. The proposition that what was largely formulated in the nineteenth century is right for the twenty-first must be tested in open debate.

There have been some excesses in recent teaching methods and they can be damaging, but we cannot allow them to block legitimate positive innovation provided that it is properly monitored and validated. There is much talk in the United States of America of the need to step outside existing teaching methods and look for completely fresh alternatives. We have the advantage of a defined curriculum base from which to do the same.

There must be what in Scotland would be a not proven verdict on the subject-centred structure of the national curriculum. Academic theses abound on the origins, power, and longevity of the subject tradition. They are pretty well divided on the merits of the case. Do subjects exist to enable learning or as a vehicle for vested interests, lobbies, and departmental baronies? In my view, the national curriculum was pretty well bound to go the way that it did. The weight of tradition and political imperatives came together over public suspicion about the alternatives such as teaching children through their own experience. They did not sound strong and were open to charges of watering-down the curriculum.

The ten subjects were inevitable and were probably right in terms of restoring public confidence by playing to existing strengths. They had, for some, the added bonus of moving away from the professionals, not least HMI, sounding like a move away from trendy meddling and back to basics: there would be no room for soft options like drama or dance!

On the whole, the national curriculum has not worked out too badly – so far. Implementation and testing have both been much assisted by building on existing practice. Efforts to reconcile the national curriculum have not been entirely unavailing, and room has been found within the whole curriculum framework for the other essential ingredients which constitute a real education. Despite recent criticism, technology remains a huge bonus: the remarkable extra ingredient. Not only has it brought relevance and a closer rapport with industry, it has and will question and loosen subject boundaries, demonstrating that concepts, skills, and thought processes transcend them. It will enable these skills to be identified wherever they are in the national curriculum and to be mapped systematically, and to forge core skills in post-16 education. There are some gloomy reports about how it is faring just now. It has the strength to prevail in the long run.

The scope which the 1988 Education Reform Act gives to schools to organise the curriculum components in their own way has yet to be exploited. As I have argued many times, it is possible for schools to throw the attainment targets in a heap on the floor and reassemble them in the way that best meets their needs. Much overload and overlap could be eliminated, and period bells could be declared redundant. That step does not appear to have been taken, but there are signs that as schools begin to feel at ease with the system they may explore the freedom which is theirs for the taking.

Where developments have not been so rigidly constrained there is a tendency to introduce flexibility. In many respects, the Northern Ireland curriculum is a Mark 2 version of the English – almost the one we might have had given more time and professional involvement in the planning. Flexibility has averted many of the problems of overcrowding and over-prescription. It could be that the Welsh will go the same way: although starting with a curriculum even more crowded by the addition of Welsh Language, they are by dint of applied common sense, and not a little panache, pace-setting in ways which England would do well to emulate.

There may well be developments which lessen the subject stranglehold as time goes by. That is not to imply their demise, but a search for balance between the best interests of pupils – who will not go out into a world neatly divided into subjects – and the subject disciplines and feelings and attitudes of society. Any political will to prevent this would require further legislation.

The rush to revise mathematics and science in order to reduce the attainment targets to accommodate the GCSE may, at the expense of making many curriculum plans in schools obsolete, reduce the complications if not the content. More significantly, it will now be virtually impossible to revise them again for some years. As a result, worthwhile changes based on experience may have to wait longer than they should. The working group reports may have been state-of-the-art in 1988 but four years on there is room for trimming, rearranging, and clarifying.

There is, more controversially, a strong case for a review in English as the final report was less specific on reading and grammar than it should have been. While the mathematics working group agreed that there was room for both the modern and the traditional such as problem-solving and long division, the English group was not so explicit in saying that while pupils can learn grammar in context, they can also benefit from a more traditional systematic approach. It is tempting to think that in reading, more precise guidance in a range of methods, together with more explicit attainment targets, might have forestalled some of the more extreme debate and controversy. Political opportunism has generated infinitely more heat than light; education is ill-suited for shooting from the hip.

History and geography are prime examples of subject lobbies getting too much in, with their conclusions distorted for political purposes. It will be wise to let them be, benefit from experience of implementation, and to evaluate before applying the knife. The same applies to art and music. If they are to become the practical subjects which most people expect them to be, then there must be a realistic trimming of the knowledge content, the clearest example of the right-wing push towards acquiring knowledge rather than skills.

In a changing world, it seems quaintly out of touch to go down this path. That is not to deny knowledge and understanding, simply to plead for balance. Industry rightly calls for the basic skills of numeracy and literacy, for practical adaptable skills before a body of potentially out-of-date knowledge.

It is common, but futile, to lament the debasement of education to the status of political football. With its new-found pre-eminence as being crucial to national survival that is as inevitable as the amount of attention now being paid to primary schools and whether or not they can teach the basic skills of reading, writing and arithmetic. The state of play in primary education is endemically obscure, making it a natural subject for debate as we wait to see what difference the national curriculum will make.

As is their wont, the staffs of primary schools have, in the face of much discouragement, performed miracles. Their rewards have been to be in the thick of a pretty unrewarding debate on standards. Every generation claims in the teeth of evidence that things have gone from bad to worse. The worst that one can say, based on the evidence, is that they have remained much the same, with no dramatic changes to justify the furore.

If there is little evidence that standards are too high, there is even less for the reverse. NCC found, as did HMI, that schools, if anything, spent too much time on the basics, and not enough on breadth. Most employ a variety of teaching methods. The first monitoring exercise confirmed the beginning of a rise in standards, but not that they were worryingly low.

The national curriculum inevitably raised the question of resources, which have risen significantly for in-service training. Those for books and equipment have not. The changes have also thrown the two issues of class sizes and specialist teaching for 10- and 11-year-olds into stark relief. While class sizes continued to decline, however slowly, little attention was paid to the additional demands of the new curriculum. When pupil–teacher ratios started to climb, however, the time had come for NCC to dig into its data and pronounce on the significance of the class size changes. Regrettably, it has not. It is a subject close to many hearts. When parents are asked what changes would most improve education they invariably say class sizes should be smaller. But smaller than what? There is no definite, optimum class size. Such evidence as there is suggests that the ideal pupil–teacher ratio is not one to one. Adults who had individual tutors or governesses when young will testify to that: siblings play as significant a part in education as adults. Below a certain number, probably about 15, pupils start to lose the class dynamic that broadens experience and stimulates competition. Everybody accepts that class sizes can be too big. Most people, especially those with children of primary age, worry about anything over 30. In my experience, 25 is about the right number, assuming that classes are not mixed-age, where the spread of ability and maturity poses additional problems for teachers. Practical considerations underpin the debate. Of crucial importance is the time a teacher can devote to each pupil for personal support, assessment, perceptual difficulties and encouragement, and on marking and correcting: the more meticulously this is done, the better for the child.

The national curriculum is based on the assumption that pupils, individually or in groups, will be at different levels in each subject and will progress at different speeds. While whole-class teaching has its place, a part of each day must be reserved for group and individual teaching. The bigger the class, the harder this becomes. Traditionalists say the answer is to revert to chalk and talk, claiming that then it does not matter what size the class is. Not too many parents would warm to this, and rightly so.

Schools have to cope with the fact that in few places do parents collectively contrive to produce offspring in neat groups of 25 of each age. It follows that some classes will be bigger than average, some smaller. Heads must also try to make classes smaller at the infant rather than at the junior stage – and that is not easy.

There is no good educational reason for class sizes to start rising again. If 25 seems a sensible sort of level, the existence of too many classes of more than 30 is not good news for pupils, parents, teachers, or the delivery of the national curriculum. Class size, however, is not everything. Research from the National Foundation for Educational Research has shown that classroom management is important too, but even greater expertise in that cannot buy the time which delivery of the national curriculum demands.

It is difficult to know what to make of the demands for more specialist teaching at the upper end of the primary school. The report of the so-called Three Wise Men in January 1992 was a flawed mixture of good practice, assertion, and political expediency. How much of the talk of specialism was politically inspired and was it educationally sound? The arguments must be as strong for extending primary methods upwards into secondary schools – as so many successful middle-schools do – as for the introduction of earlier specialisation.

Before we rush off into change, there is an urgent need for a cool appraisal of all the arguments. If NCC is to fulfil its broader remit it should commission objective investigation of both this and class sizes. NCC must undertake the work because it is unlikely that ministers will, and governors faced with allocating priorities within tight budgets will need to know the relative strengths of the arguments for smaller classes against equipment, accommodation, and so on.

The introduction of the national curriculum continues to highlight its incompatibility with the GCSE. This is not to denigrate either. Due to accidents of timing and the existence of hermetically sealed stables in the establishment, initiatives appeared which had absolutely nothing in common. Politically, the GCSE had to be supported, even though it was suspected of being less rigorous than the GCE it replaced. The new examination's striking success in terms of results stems from its radicalism: it set out to capture a broader market of 16-year-olds than ever before, to be more than a step for the few on the ladder to university. It is designed to celebrate success not delineate failure.

The figures speak for themselves: more stay on post-16; more than 30 per cent of passes are at Grades A to C. Naturally, it is now criticised as being too easy with the amount of course-work getting the blame and there is to be a new top grade to match the heights of level 10 of the national curriculum. It is hard to see what benefit able pupils will derive from this, while the status of the existing A and lower grades will be diminished. The changes will emphasise the terminal feel which this type of examination generates, especially when externally marked.

The system, so long in gestation, is an anachronism in an age when continuity matters and the need is for clear credits which will carry real weight in further education. The course-work/modular approach, which is the strength of GCSE, could be put to more appropriate use in a system based on the national curriculum and designed for continuity from 14 to 19. The more explicit information provided by national curriculum assessment properly recorded in a comprehensive Record of Achievement would assuredly encourage more youngsters to acquire credits which could be used in later education or training and be of infinitely more use to employers than bald GCSE grades in separate subjects.

One has to look hard to find other countries with external terminal examinations for 16-year-olds. In Scotland, there are proposals for them to be replaced by equivalent examinations at 15, to be flexible, and to be internally assessed. In England, we too must come to trust schools to carry out key stage 4 assessment at 16. It is not difficult to envisage a day when schools could gain the right to assess in their own name, with the minimum of external moderation. The practice appears to work well in parts of the United States. Until then, a more formal system based on the excellent Business and Technician Education Council (BTEC) one could operate. The financial savings would be massive, perhaps at the expense of the examination board industry. Teachers could be seen to be trusted and 14–19 continuity and incentives enhanced. Problems of monitoring are there to be solved, not to be used as a pretext for inertia and lack of imagination. The changes would require a degree of honesty that may not be forthcoming and it is to the credit of Angela Rumbold, the former Minister of State in the Baker regime, that she was one of the first to sense the need for examination changes along these lines. It is to be hoped that the case can be made and sustained, based on a renewed trust in schools and teachers. That trust could surely allow for the resolution of the arid and polarised debate about course-work and testing through written examinations. At times, the debate appears to have a moral base, portrayed as a choice between good and evil. We need a range of testing mechanisms.

Course-work assessment, often of modules, has a long and respectable history in industry and the services, and increasingly in higher education. It motivates – clear targets and attainable time-spans work with able as well as less able students. It is akin to life experience. It rewards consistency and perseverance and is the only sensible way of assessing practical work.

Formal testing has its place, too. It places value on cumulative knowledge, a steady nerve, and positive response to pressure. It is self-evident that a combination of the two will combine many strengths. But the argument has become trivialised, caricatured by political debate and tradition versus trendy liberalism. An image of high stools and quill pens and an odd sense of moral rectitude attach to testing, which panders to the public's gut reaction. There is evidence that the public preference for formal testing is growing, particularly amongst those with no formal qualifications. If this is so, it is even more important that the arguments for course-work and modules should not go by default. Ministers should know better: theirs is not to pander but to lead and England does have a great deal of catching up to do: it is still the country which does least for its less able children.

Moving on to A-levels, I recall an occasion when immediately after a speech by Kenneth Clarke reaffirming the examination as the educational gold standard, I was called upon by a group of visiting educationists from abroad to explain why he seemed to think that we were the envy of the world. Try it as an off-the-cuff exercise! At times it has seemed as if it was – and is – the last stand of a sinking, embattled enclave determined to hold on at any cost to a system and a label for its own sake. Defections have been frequent since the Higginson Report advocated five leaner A-levels to replace the narrow diet of three which still has the potential to produce illiterate scientists and innumerate literati.

The A-level examination is a sheep and goats system par excellence, standing four-square in the way of any genuine attempt to bridge the academic and vocational divide. However impressive and well-intentioned the efforts to provide a co-ordinated pattern of post-16 education, it will not be possible while parity of esteem is blocked by failure to accept that the A-level system has to be changed. One way, though less than satisfactory, would be to put both academic and vocational qualifications on to the same gold standard. Not surprisingly, a suggestion that the general National Vocational Qualification should be given a user-friendly title such as 'vocational A-level' was greeted with undisguised horror by ministers. More likely to be effective would be a fundamental change, based on the recognition that academic and vocational cannot be separately defined – how, for example, can there be an A-level in law? – particularly when a consequence is that around 30 per cent of those who embark on academic A-level courses fail to gain anything. The waste and the heartache are monumental, particularly when set against an un-impressive staying-on rate which has winnowed out potential students even before the starting gate.

Of all the topics in which I was involved in discussions, the debates on the future of A-levels were second only in irrationality to the early argu-ments over key stage 4. Rational argument was met with unsubstantiated assertion and, sadly, an implication that treason was afoot. It is possible to change, to improve, while not jeopardising standards. Even if in practice A-levels do encapsulate all that we ever need, they cannot, surely, uniquely encapsulate it. Like a Rolls-Royce, they are impressive, with few modifications, and aimed at a fairly limited market. Imagine what would happen to innovation of any kind if it was attacked on the premise that what we have is so good that we cannot change it for fear of diluting it.

It was, and is, tiresome to see long overdue change opposed sim-plistically as a threat to existing standards. One meeting that stands out in my memory was when we came to discuss the introduction of core skills for all 16- to 19-year-olds including A-level students, a commonplace abroad and soon to be in place north of the border. The proposal was dismissed at the highest level on the grounds, manifestly absurd, that all A-levels already embodied all the skills *per se*, and would be diluted by meddling. It was surprising to learn that studying A-level English generated *per se* extension of numeracy.

Too much of what passes as A-level studies is based on academic traditions, the education of an elite, and the acquisition of knowledge for its own sake. While the narrowness can be redeemed by good general studies courses, their incidence is too random and their quality too variable for them to be a reliable antidote. Despite all the efforts genuinely made by SEAC against the odds to make them a constructive broadening influence, we all know that Advanced Supplementary levels are a failure as they stand and in no sense address the academic/vocational question.

NCC has a statutory responsibility for 16–19 education in schools. Behind the scenes, members were much exercised by questions such as if there was a national curriculum at pre-16, why was there nothing com-parable and appropriate at post-16? The *de facto* position is that the curr-iculum is defined purely in terms of individual examination syllabuses. The council thought it was important that it should attempt a suitable modified and tentative whole-curriculum post-16, particularly by exten-sion of the dimensions, skills, and themes embodied in *Curriculum Guidance 3*. The messages from ministers and civil servants were un-mistakably clear – the definition is self-evident. At times it was implied that the post-16 curriculum was exclusively a matter for SEAC, which, to its credit, did not share that view.

The vocational examination bodies have attempted to provide a common background to specific studies, certainly as far as skills are concerned. NCC's work on the definition of core skills, directed at A- and AS-level students, has been taken up, developed, and refined by the vocational sector. The proposals now being considered in Scotland are based on a similar assumption of an underlying pattern guaranteeing a common base, just one of the proposed ways of facilitating transfers between tracks which are both general and vocational, albeit with different emphases.

In England there are other gaps yet to bridge, not least that between narrow competence or work-based skills, and the broader skills advocated by NCC and the BTEC. The general national vocational qualification (NVQ) may solve the problem. With a fair wind, it might storm the A-level citadel which is so tenuously, if obdurately, defended. In any case, England must take increasing cognisance of the very different but related patterns in the rest of Europe. On this occasion at least, it would be a mistake to perpetuate the practice of holding the Scottish system of education in the highest disregard.

It could be a long time before there is a satisfactory scheme for examinations at 16 and 19 as we do not yet seem to be clear where the starting and finishing points are. As regards testing at 7, 11, and 14, it is easier to predict. Testing at 14 could go a number of ways. Under the influence of the examination board tradition, it could become a sort of pre-GCSE, or it could become a means of substituting for GCSE a national curriculum-based assessment for pupils before they embark on the 14–19 section of their education, hopefully with fewer discontinuities than now. If schools are trusted more and more with the assessment it could be handled imaginatively and more constructively than externally marked testing can be. Teachers would, it goes without saying, need to give more positive reassurances than they have so far that they and the national curriculum can do something to shift the culture of under-achievement and under-expectation which still dogs the system. There are still echoes of the 1980s intransigence among the unions which is so damaging to the restoration of trust.

As far as testing at the ages of 7 and 11 is concerned, the moves towards a progressively simplified system will continue, if only because it is not possible either to validate by research the results of a system as complicated as that envisaged by the Task Group on Assessment and Testing (TGAT) in 1989, nor possible to resource it in terms of financial or staff costs. In any case, as many experienced local government administrators pointed out at the time, the logistics of the system do not add up: it is simply too fraught with complications of scale and time. One way to illustrate this is by reference to the government-sponsored report on the 1991 standard assessment tasks (SATs) of 7-year-olds. Laying aside that it was shelved between its completion in December 1991 and the election in April 1992, and that it brought the league tables into disrepute, the report

127

by Leeds University revealed that training for teachers in the administration of the tests varied so widely throughout the country that they were
unable to carry through the tests in conformity with the procedures laid
down to ensure nation-wide validity. Some teachers were said to be so
unsure of what they were doing that they gave everyone two marks out
of three. NCC could have told the government so. In short, the Leeds
report was conclusive proof that if you set out to be over-ambitious,
Murphy's law of diminishing returns and sod's law that if it can go wrong
it will, combine to deal a death blow to the integrity of the grand design.
There is also the odd Conservative law that the more you underfund
something the better it will work.

The battle will be over the nature of the simplified tests. Political and,
to an extent, public – as distinct from parental – instinct will be to go for
simple, controllable tests, formally administered and comfortingly
familiar. These will tend to produce a system which measures institutions
rather than pupils, measures tangibles rather than skills and concepts, and
takes us back to testing weaknesses rather than strengths. The diagnostic
value of the tests will tend to be diminished and their role in classifying
and categorising enhanced. No wonder there is an overwhelming atmosphere of *déjà vu* about. The ultimate manifestation of these are crude,
unweighted league tables. Unfortunately, in order to perform well in such
tables, a school has to consider whether to compromise the interests of
individuals, either by excluding them from the school entirely – giving a
whole new meaning to the concept of choice – or, in the case of examinations such as GCSE, by preventing all but cast-iron-pass potential pupils
from entering. The more simplistic the test, the more negative the outcomes. This is not to argue against simple testing or assessing, quite the
reverse: they have their place. It is an argument against over-ambitious
expectations from testing, trying to extend their use beyond the needs of
the pupil and the maintenance and improvement of standards, and
against imposing a system based on the fond beliefs that the only valid
tests are the ones inflicted on past generations.

If one were to set out again on the quest for a means of testing the
outcomes of the national curriculum, with perhaps more thought, less
prejudice, and a greater awareness of the nature of the beast, I suggest one
would come closer still to what I said to Kenneth Baker shortly after I was
appointed. The national curriculum is much more important than the
testing – being able to drive a car is more important than passing a driving
test; the curriculum must lead the testing. What the testing should seek to
achieve is, in ascending order of importance: pressure upon teachers and
schools to reach a uniform higher standard, more accurate information for
parents about the development potential and progress of their offspring,
and clear diagnostic information to enable the most appropriate programme of support for each individual pupil, tailored to his or her needs.

In addition, and the testing system has this much to its credit, assessing children's progress against a defined yardstick is now accepted as being valuable. It will be interesting to compare and contrast what actually happens with these simple criteria. Teachers will have to be well aware that supporting steps which appear to cut down on their workload can be double-edged weapons. Parents will have to make it clear, as they always have done when asked, that positive information on their own child, revealing strengths as well as weaknesses, is far more important than a fine set of national statistics. It is easy to be misled.

I well remember the case of the Suffolk Reading Tests. The norm was 100; each year the average tended to rise until it was 112. Each year education committee members congratulated themselves that standards were rising. Somehow it hardly seemed helpful to tell them that the tests simply needed recalibrating! Likewise, when Kenneth Clarke bemoaned the first results of the reading SATs for 7-year-olds on the grounds that 25 per cent or so were below average he seemed to show a calculated ignorance of the meaning of averages – 50 per cent or so were around average and the other 25 per cent were above it – what else could he expect. I suspect that it demonstrates not so much ignorance, as a wilful distortion for political ends. A proper evaluation of standards is going to become increasingly difficult as there is little independent statistical evidence available since the politicisation of NCC and SEAC and the emasculation of HMI. These bodies should also have something to say about the future of teacher training. Knocking it might arguably be the second oldest pastime, but the proposal to shift 80 per cent (now reduced to 65 per cent) of it to schools smacked of the fundamentalist tendency to find simplistic solutions to complex problems. As far as the national curriculum is concerned, it is not possible to see how, in the remaining space, students can be inducted into the arcane mysteries of attainment targets, statements, strands, programmes of study, SATs, etc. without divine intervention. If this is to be achieved in schools instead, then most teachers would, I think, confess to a fear of the partially blind having to lead the totally blind. How inefficient it must seem, and how far removed from achieving a national approach, to have penny numbers of embryo teachers gaining their basic training in logistics and content in some schools and staffrooms we can all think of.

There is a strong case for a national curriculum for teacher training hammered out in partnership between government, teacher trainers and schools. As so often, it is a matter of achieving the right balance and what can best be done by whom, where. Some thought should, in particular, be devoted to how training can be carried on through the first vital year in school after training. A great strength of the proposed entry grade for new teachers, rejected as too costly by government, was a lightened teaching load, combined with additional formal training. If quality is the goal, the costs in cash terms were insignificant.

I wish to conclude this chapter on a note of idealism. This may seem to strike a jarring note, one not in accord with the times. Times were when idealism was a prime motivating force for change, particularly in education. The great Education Acts from Forster's to Butler's were aimed at broadening the constituency which would have the privilege of access. They mirrored the Parliamentary Reform Acts in that sense.

At the centre of idealism is a measure of selflessness, a feeling that both community and every individual within it matters and that the former is more than an aggregration of self-interests. It is interesting to contemplate how the 'Great' Education Reform Act of 1988 measures up. In a sense, it echoes the strains of the Thatcherite theme: how could it be else? And yet, in the preamble, worth repeating, appear these words:

> The governing body and head teacher of every maintained school
> are required to provide a curriculum which:
> - is balanced and broadly based
> - promotes the spiritual, moral, cultural, mental and physical development of pupils at the school and of society
> - prepares pupils for the opportunities, responsibilities and experiences of adult life
> - includes religious education for pupils of statutory school age

Whether or not they were a last minute insertion by a shrewd civil servant, they lend respectability and hope. So did the implicit entitlement which a national curriculum could confer. Played with determination, here was a counter to the divisiveness of other trends in society and in education. It is difficult to reconcile the harsher aspects of the market-force philosophy with a tradition of education as the gateway to a life of opportunity where inequalities at the starting gate are taken into account. Even with the best of intentions, education has stubbornly remained the prerogative of the middle classes. The best guarantee is to be born in the right place with the right parents and with a silver spoon in the mouth.

Tom Sobell, the far-seeing director of education in New York said, chillingly, when last in Britain that, in spite of all the efforts, under-privilege still corresponds with under-achievement. This is not, of course, just Britain's problem. To many here, though, it seemed that the national curriculum would bring positive change with its implications for stand-ards, expectations, and entitlement. That was certainly the key reason behind my decision to accept the chairmanship at NCC, even if I was not entirely convinced that the government shared similar aspirations.

In practical terms what was on offer? First of all, the national curri-culum was for all, and that meant the least able, the most disadvantaged, just as much as the gifted. The vast majority of those consulted in 1989 by NCC were opposed to exemption and exclusion. NCC nailed its colours firmly to the mast. Although the problems this brave decision created were, and are, formidable, new hopes and enthusiasms were kindled amongst parents and teachers of the handicapped, and the benefits of being clearly and unequivocally in the mainstream are now plainly seen. Horizons have broadened and aspirations have been raised.

Considerable ingenuity was applied by NCC into making the attainment targets attainable by all; in their original form certain pupils were inadvertently excluded by the wording. Without setting double standards, it was found possible to allow for a wide range of communications as best suited to individual pupils. Only from specifics such as those requiring the free motor skills of handwriting was exemption seen as the answer. It was emphasised that time was not of the essence in making progress, as long as the assessment process was sensitive enough to reveal the relatively small steps needed to indicate achievement. At the same time, it has been made clear that token claims that pupils are working within the national curriculum do pupils no service. There is a danger of tokenism which must be recognised and resisted. SEAC responded positively to NCC requests that formal assessment should be as sensitive as possible.

Even as early as 1989, NCC expressed concern that assessment arrangements for pupils with special educational needs should not lead to adverse judgements being made about schools. NCC adopted the motto 'minorities are a privilege, not a problem'. Research is now overdue into how things have worked out for pupils with permanent or temporary special needs. Has the initial fillip and all the dedicated work of NCC committees and teachers borne fruit? It may well be that resource constraints have diminished much of what might have been achieved. Certainly it is true that after its initial publication on guidance, NCC was limited in its resources to undertake or commission the wide-ranging work which is necessary.

Work commissioned from the Cambridge Institute of Education in 1990 has led to the production, in 1992, of *Curriculum Guidance 9 – The national curriculum and pupils with severe learning difficulties*, which deals with English, mathematics and science and is a welcome supplement to the excellent work undertaken in many schools. *Curriculum Guidance 10*, also published in 1992, gives assistance to pupils with special educational needs in science. The potential is still there: at least the right to access can be demanded by teachers and parents with statutory backing.

The national curriculum picture is less satisfactory when it comes to equal opportunities. Looking at equal opportunities in their broadest meaning, it is hard to conclude other than that the years since 1988 have seen a decline in equality in education as in other areas of society for those who need the most help. There is, for example, no longer positive discrimination in favour of schools that are in under-privileged areas such as some of the deprived inner-city areas. Local education authorities have in recent years, through a mixture of cut-backs and reforms in the funding of schools, lost the freedom with budgets which made this possible. As parental contributions towards the costs of essentials have risen, so have the inequalities between provision in 'have' and 'have-not' areas. Self-evidently, schools in relatively well-to-do areas are better equipped than those in run-down districts, often thanks to parents' fund-raising activities or direct contributions. The contrasts, always disturbing to the visitor, are now painful to witness.

The potential is none the less there for governing bodies to work out quite accurately the costs of delivering the national curriculum, and to shift funds to where they see the real needs in their schools. On a brighter note, there is encouraging evidence that in terms of the curriculum, the requirements do guarantee a norm not there before. This must certainly be true as regards gender. The national curriculum requirement in science means that at last girls will not go for, or be eased towards, Biology and boys to physics. Technology has to become pretty distorted before girls are excluded from broader design work and boys from home economics. While the battle is far from won to remove the stereotypes, solid progress has been made.

The same has been true as regards multicultural education. There were demands from many quarters, and within NCC, for separate guidance. The debate raged as to whether the job of NCC was to make equal opportunities an ever-present, intrinsic aspect of its work, or to lead a crusade. Not without internal tension, it chose the former course. Others will judge if that was correct. What must be said was that it was made starkly clear to NCC by ministers that whatever influence it might have would be rapidly dissipated by entering what was widely seen as a no-go area. Perhaps expectations were too high amongst those affected and the pressure groups so active in the field. Certainly, NCC has conscientiously sought to remove inequality and gender-bias from each subject tackled. Often, this was unobtrusive and in detail. There was no response to the clamour for specific documents and guidance.

With hindsight, NCC might have been more courageous, not least because it was probably damned whatever it did. Where it was clearly correct, in my view, was in its insistence that the national curriculum must be studied and assessed in English. While knowledge of other mother tongues could present problems, they are best seen as a potential enrichment. Where pupils are potentially disadvantaged, then extra resources are required.

The national curriculum is a potent tool for change and for bringing about equality of opportunity. Its potential is largely unrealised as yet. It is the engine which can deliver raised standards, expectations, and greater relevance. It must be given time, not be subjected to meddling change, and should be the object of much greater scrutiny before revision is contemplated. The national curriculum's potential to underpin a revised higher education structure is enormous as it is more closely based on the needs of the average youngster and those of industry and society than is the latter. Realistically assessed, with a clear recognition that testing does not itself guarantee standards, it is there to fulfil national aspirations. The change is so fundamental that as it becomes clearer, the faint hearted will tend to take fright.

12

UNDER NEW MANAGEMENT

The National Curriculum Council and the School Examinations and Assessment Council are now under new managements. The significant changes are not in personalities but in the backgrounds to appointments. Whatever criticisms were made of Philip Halsey or myself, neither of us was widely accused of being party *apparatchiks*. The same was true of the membership of both councils in the early years. It will be interesting to see how they fare now particularly with the proposals for a merger.

It could be argued that being closer to ministers and therefore becoming more politically attuned could be an advantage. Against that must be set the obvious problems relating to the perceived independence of advice or thinking, which was difficult enough to sustain in the past. There are signs that the new chairmen are just as likely to be left stranded when political imperatives change; they may well now know that feeling which comes when the music stops and they are left holding the parcel. Two examples inevitably remain in the mind.

By altering the committee system to exclude a wide range of professional advice as part of its ongoing work and consultation, NCC appeared publicly exposed when it chose to give advice to the then Secretary of State, Kenneth Clarke, on music and art. Such bodies carry conviction when they gainsay the advice of subject working groups only when the quality of their in-house advice and their intelligence-gathering processes are beyond reproach.

Life cannot be easy for what has been a highly talented professional staff. One hopes that they can maintain their integrity in difficult circumstances. In the past, with the exception of science, NCC chose to give a lead only where views were divided and based on all the evidence available, but on the art and music recommendations there was a very significant shift in the balance. The working groups had seen art and music as practical subjects, making music being more important than learning facts about composers – and 80 per cent of those consulted agreed. So does the

Curriculum Council for Wales. Was NCC really in a minority of one or was it 'set up' to test the briskness of the reaction and allow the Secretary of State to appear conciliatory when he gave way a little, leaving NCC stranded?

Equally disturbing was the case of SEAC research on the testing for 7-year-olds in 1991, ready in December but suppressed until after the election. When it all came out, the Secretary of State could not be seen for dust, and the hapless chairman was there to carry the can.

The integrity of both bodies needs to be re-established and refurbished if they are to be able to make courageous decisions which carry conviction. Objective information is at a premium just now, and it is in everybody's interest that NCC and SEAC are free to provide it and have it accepted for what it is. Similarly, there is a dearth of open debate as a prelude to policy initiatives, and the two councils must reassert their important role as leaders of debate and holders of the ring. Whether they can continue to do this as separate bodies is as open a question as it was when they were set up. The arguments must have been finely balanced then. There is little doubt that civil servants, if not ministers, had seen with relief the Schools Council's abolition by Sir Keith Joseph as the demise of an over-mighty quango. Officials, at least, would not relish facing up to another, and divide and rule may have been uppermost in their minds. More legitimately, there was certainly the formidable size of the agenda in 1988. It amply justified the existence of two bodies with separate primary aims. If it was so then, it is not now.

In spite of all the speculation to the contrary, the two bodies worked well together – often disappointing those who were anxious for a sniff of scandal. But in truth, curriculum and assessment are inextricably linked. Some of the major issues relating to testing, course-work, GCSE assessment, and the key stage 4 saga might have been more happily resolved without tripartite involvement. But there are other players in the field, not least the National Council for Vocational Qualifications (NCVQ). If the academic/vocational gulf is to be bridged, and surely it must be, then there is every reason for combining SEAC and NCVQ. This was the option taken by New Zealand with some success in similar circumstances and has been mooted in Scotland.

There is no conceptual argument against a union of all three. Confusion as to who did what would be removed at a stroke, the flow of bumph would hopefully be stemmed, and a seamless robe could be stitched into place. This would, one suspects, lead to certain unease within Sanctuary House, the new headquarters of the Education Department, which views all quangos as bad enough but super quangos beyond contemplation. It might be better to have none of them and expand the DFE instead. However hot the denials, that would have attractions as the ultimate victory of interventionism by a department once taunted by the now defunct Manpower Services Commission for its powerlessness. I believe, however, that it will only be feasible to combine two of the three, with the more compelling being a merged SEAC and NCVQ taking over the nuts and bolts revision of the national curriculum with safeguards to ensure that curriculum interests come well before testing considerations. The only argument against that would be to preserve the separateness of A-levels at all costs. Perhaps the main obstacle is inter-departmental rivalry. Parity of esteem may well require departmental restructuring which is both real and symbolic, so we may yet end up with a Department of Education and Training, although no change followed the 1992 election apart from a cosmetic name change for the erstwhile Department of Education and Science to the Department for Education.

What then of NCC? At the most negative, there could be a case for its simple abolition once introduction of the curriculum was completed. It must be tiresome to some in government to have questions raised as to the meaning and purpose of the whole curriculum, and the need for breadth and balance, not least balance between the educational in the classical sense and the conventional or utilitarian. Without NCC there would be no need to finance or tackle the consequences of objective research.

The case for retention and a change of remit, however, is infinitely stronger. In the beginning, my queries to Kenneth Baker about the longer-term future were met with assurances, genuinely given, I believe, that England must not join those countries which, like Greece and Italy, at one time or another have allowed their national curriculums to grow out-dated into tablets of stone. Baker pointed out that the remit of NCC was described in Section 14 (3) of the Act as 'to keep ALL aspects of the curriculum under review', 'to advise the Secretary of State, and, if so requested by him, to carry out programmes of research and development for purposes connected with the curriculum for schools', 'and to publish and disseminate . . . information relating to the curriculum for schools'.

Although it was to become a battle between the 'little national curriculumers' and 'the broader believers', the Act is unequivocal – the national curriculum as such is not mentioned other than in the title of the body. He further pointed to the requirements in my job specification which related to international links and comparisons, and associated himself with my vision of NCC as a national source of excellence, above the day-to-day political fray in some aspects of its work, looking further ahead than the brief tenure of Secretaries of State and Treasury plans.

It was on that prospectus that NCC was set up, high calibre staff attracted, and long-time career prospects, if not guaranteed, then under-written. The move to York was sanctioned on that basis as was the 25-year lease of Albion Wharf headquarters. Further, the structure of NCC submitted to and approved by the DFE, the Treasury, and ministers was fashioned to meet both short- and long-term objectives.

Times change and nothing is immutable, particularly in the world of quangos – there are and have been other NCCs. None the less it was with a sense of bitter betrayal that I saw within a year the first implications of impermanence becoming manifest. The minutes of NCC are littered with assurances from ministers that the body did have a future. When a public body needs to ask such questions, the portents are ominous.

The protracted struggle over NCC's remit with respect to research was the symbol of the battle for survival. Clearly, there are many ways of tackling research in education – one does not necessarily need a National Curriculum Council to do that, but it seems perverse to spend public money to establish one, and then have an instant change of mind. The demise of NCC's role in research and of NCC itself would not be of monumental concern were it not for the fact that no alternative arrangements have been made, and it is not difficult to work out why.

Many of the political initiatives in education in the last five years have been just that – political, not buttressed by research evidence, still less by pilot schemes. They continue to contrast markedly with the priorities of parents, who insist on putting mundane things like class-sizes, adequate numbers of teachers, textbooks, and well-maintained buildings at the top of their shopping list.

The reasons for a lack of research can be briefly summarised. The main block has unquestionably been political. Even the word is suspect – hence the coded use of evaluation and monitoring. Researchers, like teachers, are politically suspect. They are seen to retain outmoded views on egalitarianism, blended with idealism. In my experience, the charge, at least to some extent, sticks. Rather too many of them have an agenda which militates against objectivity.

Research for its own sake is another endemic danger: research in education has, in my view, had a fairly low strike-rate when it comes to influencing and improving the delivery of the service on the front line. Timescales can be long, conclusions obscure at best. The bold decision to employ subject working groups rather than commission research when setting up the national curriculum seems to have been justified – embarrassingly so for the establishment. We are further on than we might have been. Having conceded that, there is another side to the argument. Under severe financial constraint and with tightly prescribed remits, the research industry, rather like teacher training, has made great but unheralded strides forward, and there are many examples of valid, practical applied research around.

When NCC in 1991 commissioned some rather circumscribed work in English, mathematics and science, stipulating that the end product had to be capable of classroom implementation without the need for interpreters, the successful bids from Warwick, King's College, and Liverpool were highly impressive. Other examples are the work of Cambridge

Institute on teacher appraisal and pupils with severe learning difficulties, and Leeds on science. There are sufficient examples to make the arguments that researchers cannot deliver unconvincing. I think it must be fear of what they might uncover which lies at the heart of the problem. The right-wing think tanks are at their most vulnerable if their policies are systematically analysed, and their pressure on ministers responsible for research, such as Angela Rumbold and Tim Eggar, was tangible and severe.

Other obstructions lie in the DFE which would naturally like to continue its practice of controlling research programmes itself – co-ordinating is a word much used in defence of their stance. There are arguments for this, but government departments are close to political pressure and tend to have more immediate priorities in terms of budget constraint: it is not the way of civil servants to take risks that might not come off.

As civil servants have come more and more into the front line of curriculum management, ministers have come to view them in the same suspicious way as they see educational professionals. I believe that it is right for the Education Department to control the overall budget, co-ordinate without suppressing and commission in areas which are administrative as distinct from curricular. But an independent budget must be elsewhere. Inexorably, that brings us back to NCC. It is there, it has the staff, and unrivalled expertise in both the mechanics of the national curriculum and the broader picture. It has the beginnings of an international network of contacts which could lead to a less insular approach to curriculum development: no recent initiative has looked, as the Howie report in Scotland has done, at European and wider dimensions – certainly not the Three Wise Men in their primary investigation. NCC, thanks to its policy of assiduously strengthening relationships with professional bodies, local education authorities, higher education and individual schools, has the links upon which practical research could be founded quickly and economically.

The council's libraries contain a unique collection of examples of best practice which could easily make it a national resource, a centre of excellence. If the patchiness which still affects education in England is to be further diminished, then identifying, analysing and publicising good practice is crucial. Teachers do not have time to reinvent a thousand wheels a day, even if they found their personal involvement beneficial. Much more practicable would be partnership in pushing forward an agreed agenda ranging from pure research through detailed updating of attainment targets and programmes of study, to curriculum development. Accomplishing this should not require the creation of a vast empire at the Albion Wharf headquarters in York.

Contrary to popular belief, the professional staff of NCC has never exceeded the mid-twenties in number. Posts were created with the aim of providing a resource which could undertake a small amount of research and monitoring directly as a control, but which could serve as liaison between NCC and three distinct groups. One would be local authorities, provided that they survive, in particular their advisory services, together with HMI – provided that they, too, continue to exist in viable numbers – with whom the work of analysing implementation, updating and best practice in the national curriculum would go ahead. A second group would be those who undertook research commissioned by NCC and to a programme which NCC was free to devise within realistic cash limits and based on wide consultation – far from the world I knew at NCC. Every project, however small, was the subject of scrutiny, interminable delay and, when occasionally conceded, specific ministerial approval was needed, even when it lay within an agreed budget. Nothing was sanctioned which did not deal narrowly with the most basic aspects of the national curriculum. The broader implications, both for the national curriculum itself and the wider world beyond were quite definitely off limits. The third group would, of course, be teachers, through professional bodies, working groups, and individual schools in the state and independent sector. The Education Reform Act can galvanise: it cannot convert. The partnerships which perhaps had to be shattered have to be rebuilt; few, if any, teachers now believe that they have a right to own the curriculum. They have a right to share in it. All those at the centre of the national curriculum at the start shared a common belief that an exciting if unwieldy monster had to be transformed into a medium for change and improvement, brought about by a partnership between the centre with its new and powerful role and the profession which would make or break it.

Such a role for NCC has much to commend it. If mergers are in the air, then perhaps the place of the NFER should come under scrutiny. The council and the NFER have worked well together, not least on the consultations. It would be worth examining the merits of establishing the NFER as an executive wing of NCC along with parts of the Assessment for Performance Unit, and the Further Education Unit, but this could only work if NCC achieved real independence. The council's freedom of action would need to be clearly defined with a broad membership representing all those with a vested interest in standards, relevance, breadth and balance. Above all, the council must have a chairman and a chief executive who are not directly appointed by a Secretary of State, whose credentials are impeccable, and who command the respect of teachers and public alike: they must be seen to be above the political battle.

The future of NCC should be the subject of major debate. A fresh ministerial team at the DFE should inform itself of the issues, and should take a crash-course on the establishment's attitude to quangos. They should accept that unbiased information has become a scarce commodity. The annual HMI report, that ever-reliable resource, seems to be endangered; it is doubtful if the Parent's Charter will quite fill the gap.

Genuinely independent voices have tended to fade: confusion is compounded by the appearance on the scene of privately-funded bodies whose titles seem to confer upon their pronouncements an aura of academic respectability to which some have no claim. Some are not politically neutral. The quality of the research which underpins their views is suspect; too often it turns out to be assertion bolstered by prejudice put forward as a disinterested contribution to debate.

Education is far too important for the debate to be distorted by lack of dispassionate information and advice, fearlessly given, by a nationally recognised body genuinely free to investigate and pronounce. How many of today's nostrums for our perceived ills would have survived such scrutiny? A prime candidate would have been that of choice when applied to the education service. That there is a need for it is beyond dispute. The virtual exclusion of parents and governors from decision taking over many years is fact. Local education authorities have been, until relatively recently, no more responsive to public pressure than other bureaucracies. As far as catchment areas, school choice, closure and reorganisation are concerned, scant attention was paid to public opinion. It could be argued that the pressures and constraints on local authorities made this virtually inevitable. None the less, the image created was that of big brother knowing better. Where the case for closure was strong, for example, justification and explanation were perceived to be unnecessary – was it not self-evident? Schools, in their own way, frequently followed suit – not least in explaining curriculum and teaching methods. Parents could appear to be little more than peripheral adjuncts to the business of formal education, even though it takes up only 1,000 or so of the 8,760 hours a year. Parents did not have access to the Secret Garden of the curriculum, let alone a hoe or a rake.

Much has changed in both local authorities and schools, but not in time to stem a tide which flowed in sympathy with the wider political thrust for choice, consumer rights and participation, although it is likely that parents want involvement rather than the reins of management. Choice is a difficult thing. Once parents think they have a choice of school for their children, for example, it is difficult to persuade them otherwise. But what does choice mean in the education context, and who really has it? The benefits of bestowing it on one group can be detrimental to another – those in the good schools which expand beyond their resources may lose in the face of the influx. Those pupils trapped in the death throes of a less popular school will suffer.

Taxpayers have some reasons for doubt when they have to fork out for under-used plant in one school while at the same time paying for a new building down the road. Recent moves to give popular schools more capital money even when good accommodation lies empty nearby hardly equate with making the best use of limited capital resources. Not so long ago local authorities were castigated by the Audit Commission for simply retaining surplus, let alone for adding to it.

The evidence is that parental choice has diminished and that in its place has come school choice. There is a campaign to improve the rights of parents being run by the very local authority associations whose members were supposed to have been inhibiting choice in the first place. Popular schools have the luxury of choice and exercise it. They choose their intake selectively, lose pupils whose results might upset the league tables and exclude troublesome pupils with little thought as to their fate and their rights. It is entirely likely that there will be between 5 to 10 per cent of potential pupils which no school will choose to accept, no doubt leaving a kind of 'untouchables colony' for the local education authorities to worry over. What will that say about equality of opportunity? Some schools which have opted out of local authority control may take advantage of the removal of the restrictions on the schools to change their character within five years, to become grammar schools. Whatever the merits of such reversion to past glories, the effect must be a diminution of parental choice: there is little merit in a range of types of schools if access to them is restricted.

There is good reason to applaud government initiatives to introduce a wider range of types of schools, but if these include grammar schools this brings selection on ability and therefore exclusion as well. It is a fact that there are some excellent grammar schools: it is also a fact that many are surrounded by impoverished 11–16 schools. Choice is a difficult concept. The answer, as in so many other things in life, lies in achieving balance, with freedom of choice within defined circumstances made clear to parents and public. Unfortunately for the opponents of local government, this postulates a degree of planning within each locality resulting in a balanced provision. It is hard to reconcile this with the opting-out movement taken to its logical conclusion. I await with interest the residents of new estates spontaneously getting together to build and seek finance for the new schools which will assuredly be required. Bureaucrats lurk waiting for them. Genuine choice seems to me to require a local education authority in one form or another.

Having been involved in the entire saga since the first attacks on local government in the mid-1970s, it is difficult not to be bitter about much of what has happened and to question the motives. Local authorities have a long and proud tradition of managing their services well and of innovation. The minority which have performed less than satisfactorily could have been dealt with without unnecessary and unsubstantiated recriminations on the majority.

This is not the place to look back beyond 1988, but it is remarkable how the old myths survive and influence. On 13 April 1992, William Rees-Mogg wrote: 'At present there is approximately one administrator for every teacher in education and similarly bureaucratic over-management in local government.' We must be pretty brainwashed if we swallow that, but how damagingly inaccurate.

Bloodied but unbowed, local education authorities appeared in 1988 to have gained a new and worthwhile role, that of quality control, contracting amd monitoring services on an agency basis – moving from a role of detailed administration and direct provision to a more strategic 'enabling' one. There are strong arguments for this – many education officers were too immersed in detail to see the wood for the trees.

The local management of schools, which passed the day-to-day running of schools to heads and governors has been largely successful, although there have been sufficient examples of things going wrong to strengthen the argument for a monitoring and supervisory role. It left LEAs free to assume a lead role in promoting and improving performance – one which they grasped with enthusiasm.

The national curriculum would not have been introduced to such an ambitious timetable without the unstinting support of local authorities, in in-service training, in exhortation, in providing resources and, where necessary, in bearing down on individual schools. Their work in supporting the introduction of testing, whatever their reservations, was critical to testing being carried out at all. It is difficult to see how they could have made a better start in their new role: and yet it is being taken from them before their performance can be judged. Their continued existence is in doubt, their role, if they survive, a residual one, sweeping up the bits that other changes leave behind. This is a massive and wilful sacrifice of resources and people which is hard to justify on rational grounds. It is not feasible to administer to the needs of 24,000 schools from Whitehall. A funding council based on those overseeing higher and further education ones would have to top all bureaucracies known to man to succeed. All but the largest secondary schools will always need support, guidance, reassurance, and monitoring on a scale quite different from that appropriate to a polytechnic. Governing bodies cannot provide this support – they, too, need help, training, and advice. There will be a continuing local need for planning, resource auditing, and quality assurance. It is hard to see the national curriculum being delivered without a local framework to reinforce the guidance from the central bodies. As things stand, it can hardly be delivered by HMI, even if that were thought desirable.

With the political demise of local authorities and HMI there is something of a black hole in the field of quality control assurance or development – the terms are rich with semantic overtones. It cannot be delivered by the market-place except in the crudest possible way, involving schools and pupils going to the wall. My views have been shaped by 30-odd years of experience in trying to raise standards and expectations – some of it bitter. It is easier to explain how it cannot be done than how it can.

My conclusion is that the overseeing of schools can be left to no single group or interest nor to a chance amalgam of all or some of them. It cannot be left to individual institutions. These inevitably lack perspective and comparative experience, and in any case internal mechanisms in any field are open to criticism. Credibility and praise where it is due come better from outside, as do warnings about complacency. Having said that, it is equally true that the best and most effective change comes from within, provided it is externally moderated and given long-term support. Further changes and the monitoring of those changes cannot be left solely to parents and the community. Their innate common sense is constant. They can see cause and effect, where politicians can't or won't. That is why they consistently place smaller classes, more books and equipment, better-paid teachers above the more fashionable nostrums. None the less, they discourage change, settle for a norm and narrow the curriculum. They need to debate this with other groups in the process.

Nor can change be based exclusively on the results of testing and league tables. How convenient – and cheap – if it could be. It is the kind of thing that people believe should be done to others. Many derived quiet amusement from the reaction of the private sector to crude tables compiled by a newspaper. The air was thick with codicils, appendices and explanations required to give what the heads described as a true picture of selective catchment areas. Some argue for market forces and consumerism based on these tables as evidence. Those who do diminish the arguments for choice. No one would buy a family car on evidence as flimsy and one-dimensional as that. There are some things which just cannot be made simple for the convenience of political dogma.

Quality cannot be guaranteed by inspections every four years by outside agencies. To be effective, inspection and monitoring need to be part of a continuous process, based on knowledge of the track record of the school and an awareness of change and evolution within it. Snapshots are useful but can be misleading. Their crudity is an insult to those who have brought about vast, seemingly unrecognised improvements in this area over the years. *Quis custodiet custodes?* The system required to control and monitor the privateers adequately might cost more than the inspections themselves. The Act demolishing the HMI and introducing league tables should be quickly repealed and forgotten.

The job might well be done, subject to qualifications, by local authorities, although not necessarily in their present form. Much of the best work in quality assurance has come from the majority which have worked with schools and teachers, combining a constructive approach with sufficient rigour to ensure change and improvement where necessary and usually by agreement. It is ten years now since Suffolk set up a system based on a curriculum resulting from wide consultation and consensus and which embodied elements of self-appraisal, external inspection, and follow-up support. In my judgement local authorities could and should be the basis for the future. They should be put at the centre of quality control with a formalised, structured relationship with a credible professional National Inspectorate. Those of us who laboured in vain to overcome the prejudices and vested interest which have so far prevented this happening must hope for a rethink.

Quality education will also flow from teacher appraisal. Delayed and nibbled round the edges the national system may be but its essential integrity remains intact, its benefits clear, its positive powers to improve demonstrated in the pilot studies. It is tempting to believe that a combination of teacher appraisal and a national curriculum might do the trick on its own. Certainly appraisal touches many hitherto unreached parts of the system. The system drawn up by the National Steering Group in 1989 which I chaired, is robust enough to withstand attack from either unions or ministers.

There is no simple panacea. National bodies, the DFE, HMI, LEAs, governors and parents, industry and commerce, all have something to contribute, but only in partnership. The ingredients are there, it is up to government to provide the recipe. After all, the whole intention of the national curriculum is to raise standards and expectations, presumably by making best use of resources and efficient management.

An initiative worth pursuing would be based on the Accreditation of Schools. There is a danger that quality assurance mechanisms tend to be top-down: there is room for a reciprocal process based on schools which brings tangible rewards to their own efforts. The process of self-audit is beneficial in itself, draws on partnerships, and identifies best practice. It is a process which can recognise the value-added which a school achieves and which is notoriously difficult to identify; its successful conclusion gives visible public endorsement in a form which everyone can recognise. In time, it would be possible for schools to gain accreditation which would enable them to carry out more and more national curriculum assessment under licence with consequent external testing cut to the minimum necessary. The work of auditing, awarding, and re-awarding could be undertaken by local authorities, private agencies, or a combination of both.

Taking the broader view of the last few years and drawing what conclusions one can, it is easy to dwell on lost opportunities, confusions, distractions. Behind these things, which do no more than reflect the human condition, lie some real achievements and the potential for more. There is no reason now why our education/economic performance should not match the best by the next century, while preserving much of what is traditionally sound. But some things will have to change in the ways we conduct our business. That they are self-evident may not necessarily help.

There are two words sadly missing from the present government's educational vocabulary, and they are hackneyed ones – balance and partnership. They sound rather soft and indecisive words, but bear with me. Balance seems to be difficult to achieve in a political system with strong adversarial black and white traditions. Polarisation takes over good ideas and drives them to extremes. Examples abound. Lay involvement in school government is good, if based on a mutual respect for an understanding of the respective roles of layman and professional. Choice is good if it is within agreed bounds and, critically, to mutual advantage. Local management of schools is good if it does not distract heads from their main purpose and does not lead to the loss of economies of scale and efficiency. It is right to question institutions such as the DFE, local authorities, and HMI as long as one is willing to recognise their strengths, and the potential downside in terms of disruption and alternative bureaucracies if one changes them. It is right to question the role of the professional, as long as one does not discard his advice, while accepting views based on unsubstantiated prejudice and whim. The list is long, the point is simple. Everything that exists has good and bad points, every potential replacement has, too. Government can degenerate into an endless exercise in shifting boundaries. In education, most, if not all, of this is irrelevant to the needs of the pupil and the quest for standards.

Partnership is the concomitant of balance. Antagonisms exacerbate legitimate differences in points of view and lead to lack of balance. If this book demonstrates one thing it is that rivalries and old power struggles distract and distort. If all the energy that was devoted to inter-institutional rivalries and the centre had instead been devoted solely to improving what was going on in our schools, a tangible rise in standards for everybody would already be evident. Unless the juggernaut traditional power of the Civil Service machine and its formidable *esprit de corps* is tested and modified, heaven help any outsider, individual, or institution. The balance between the practices of the government machine and experience from the outside world has not yet been struck. The partnership between local and central government has been tested close to destruction. In a country without a written constitution there is arguably a greater need for a counterbalance to the centre than elsewhere. Whatever its alleged misdeeds and shortcomings, local government is too important to be cast aside as it has been. The fact that Audit Commission figures show it in the 1980s to have out-performed central government in efficiency is sufficient to fuel dark thoughts about why it has all happened.

Local education authorities are the greater part of local government: not only have their successes gone unrecognised, their unobtrusive values have seemingly been overlooked. If the decline of the authorities is at least partly due to the annexation of power by the DFE, and it must be, it would be worse if all at Sanctuary House, and not just the more perceptive, did not recognise that the loss of that partnership leaves a huge gap in day-to-day supporting and monitoring of schools. The quiet mediator, the reassuring adviser, that is what schools will miss most. The value of the partnership between schools and their local authority has been underestimated.

How will it be replaced? Will the centre fund new institutions to carry out this role? Will it treat the new bodies, presumably councils without an elective base, any different from countless other quangos? Can partnership exist if education is locally administered by extensions of central government?

I would urge the deepest and most profound thought and consultation before replacing rather than reshaping local education authorities. The alternative must be clear decisive action. A lingering death by a thousand opt-outs, the power vacuum extended, is in no-one's interest. Will the Education Department really want to know that Much Snoring Primary School's loos are frozen or that the lollipop lady is missing?

Two other partnerships also need refurbishing. The first is that between government and teacher, which will require more than a few encouraging words to put an end to the shock treatment of the past few years. Unless ideas – and power – are shared the country will not reap the benefits of the changes. That means trust. There is evidence still that teachers are not trusted to teach, to test. Whatever caused the breakdown of trust – and the extreme political and industrial action of some teachers in the 1980s must take a portion of the blame – the past must be firmly in the past for all sides. John Patten, the new Secretary of State for Education has made an encouraging start.

There will be problems, such as the recognition of differences of opinion, and the involvement of parents and local education authorities as full partners. It will – and this is equally difficult – mean the re-establishment of trust between government and the professionals in the field. Forget the individuals: the presence of the chairmen of NCC and SEAC and the chief HMI at policy meetings, at least enabled the consequences of policy changes to be spelled out. No matter that this often led to accusations of delaying tactics and the frustrating of dreams. From that friction came moderated decisions, more reasonable time-scales, and so on. In the last months of the Clarke regime, it was noticeable – for example over course-work – that the consequences for schools, teachers and children were totally overlooked.

Government must talk again to teacher trainers to enlist their help. Most of them are refreshingly free of cloven feet and horns. Nobody disputes that much teacher training should take place in school – but how much? Likewise, governments must initiate and carry through policies – but surely not without evidence of the state of play and a range of implications to ponder. Change is not without cost. A study of the rate at

146

which teachers can absorb change might have led to a more sensible timetable and at least some view as to priorities. Partnerships and consultations do not lessen government power to govern, they can enhance its effectiveness. There is no need to revert to the 'consultation as an excuse for inaction' argument – that was another manifestation of lack of balance.

With an injection of common sense and some active partnership, an agenda emerges. A balance of interests will assist towards sorting out the 16–19 academic vocational tangle. Once it can be accepted that A-levels are not perfect, and that change need not diminish standards, doors open. There is no dearth of talent amongst the interested groups. If choice is seen as valuable, but not a god, then we can begin to work out how to give the individual greater freedom without detriment to the majority.

We could recognise that choice will mean less to the depressed inner-city areas and realise that it is society that has the choice to really do something there. We could choose to preserve the best of what grammar schools offer without their potential divisiveness. If the need for national quality assurance is accepted – and it should be at a time when raising standards and expectations are so high on the agenda – we can set about creating the machinery to achieve it. Whatever machinery is set up there is little chance of private inspections surviving scrutiny; there should be the strengthening of HMI rather than its destruction; there can be no place for crude league tables. Either value-added can be brought into the equation or it can't; in the latter case, other ways of informing the parents must be hammered out.

And now the national curriculum. It may seem odd to say it, but the first warning is not to be frightened at its scope and its success. There is a difference between reducing complexity and over-prescription and abandoning whole sections of it. The key stage 4 saga may be seen in the long term to have made it a 5–14 curriculum, instead of from 5–19 as it should be. Narrowing it to the basics could be superficially appealing: easy, testable and cheap, but that is the route of the Philistines. It is true that what you test is what you get, so testing will have to broaden rather than narrow even if this does go against the gut-reaction of the Conservative right. Testing will have to be less and less externally imposed with more carried out within schools by teachers who are adequately trained and trusted. It will not be difficult to keep national yardsticks for their positive values rather than as rods to beat the backs of teachers.

The correct balance will have to be struck between making changes to the content of individual subjects in the curriculum as soon as they seem desirable and waiting until the evidence is conclusive. Ministers have erred on the side of the former so far and must resist further temptation. An independent NCC with renewed confidence should help ministers to find the correct pace of change and then to drive it through when required. The council should not allow debate between subject teaching and sensible integration to slacken. The ten subjects may be inscribed in statute – they are not in Holy Writ. The council should ensure that technology is not emasculated by the traditional subjects, and, above all, that breadth and balance matter and are maintained.

Extra-curricular work is a misnomer for much that is essential, provided that it is delivered to standards comparable with those set for statutory lessons. That implies much greater emphasis on a curriculum for all – those with special needs, minorities, pupils of all abilities. The machine in place is capable of delivering all that. Given time, and a more informed debate than those conducted at a tabloid level about reading and international league tables, it will raise standards. It needs a vote of confidence and time to deliver.

There is one great strength of the national curriculum legislation which must not be compromised. The Act insists that the organisation of the curriculum lies with the head teacher. The Secretary of State may not prescribe how much time may be spent on any particular programme of study, may not require specific ways of providing a subject in the school timetable, and will not specify teaching methods or materials. Delivery of the curriculum is for the professional not the politician, and must remain so.

Education came close to disaster in the Clarke era as he put pressure to bear on primary schools to introduce subject teaching with formal class-teaching methods. While these are legitimate areas of debate, they must be out of bounds for unilateral politicians. Teachers, with access to the best advice and research, must be allowed to take the lead in choosing the teaching methods that will bring the biggest benefit to all their pupils. If parents and the public are uneasy, then a proper public debate should take place.

A yet greater danger to a national curriculum is the improper political prescription of content, as happened with history, and in enforcing teaching methods based on prejudice. Clarke overstepped the bounds in insisting that changes were made in the content of the final orders in history and geography that were neither logically nor educationally sound. Everybody concerned about education must be alert to the dangers.

Now that a revolution has been implemented to a demanding time-scale, the most decentralised of systems has a national curriculum but it does not yet have the machinery to measure and ensure quality. That debate is hardly even under way. The solution must do justice to the national curriculum as outlined by Kenneth Baker, the Secretary of State who introduced it.

Baker told the North of England Education Conference on 6 January 1989 that the curriculum would:

- give a clear incentive for all schools to catch up with the best and the best will be challenged to do even better;

- provide teachers with detailed and precise objectives;
- provide parents with clear, accurate information;
- ensure continuity and progression from one year to another, from one school to another;
- help teachers concentrate on the task of getting the best possible results from each individual child.

On the whole it has.

GLOSSARY

Assessment arrangements: The arrangements for assessment which will demonstrate each pupil's achievement at the end of each key stage. They include a variety of assessment methods, including both testing and continuous assessment by teachers and Standard Assessment Tasks (SATs).

Attainment targets: Objectives for each foundation subject of the national curriculum, setting out the knowledge, skills, and understanding that pupils of different abilities and maturities are expected to develop. They are further defined at 10 levels of attainment by means of appropriate statements of attainment.

Basic curriculum: This comprises the national curriculum and religious education (RE).

Concepts: In history, forms of generalising and categorising content: some are 'over-arching' and common to all history (cause, effect, change, etc.); others tend to be more specific to time and place or field of study (Napoleonic, feudalism, the Reformation, Empire, technology, etc.).

Content: A word open to a range of interpretations, but usually employed to mean the information which supports a given field of study.

Core subjects: English, mathematics and science and, in relation to schools in Wales which are Welsh speaking, Welsh.

Cross-curricular themes: Strands of provision which will run through the national curriculum and may also extend into RE and provision outside the basic curriculum.

Curriculum Council for Wales (CCW): This body performs the same functions as the National Curriculum Council (NCC), but with reference to the curriculum in Wales.

Differentiation: (1) Teaching each subject at different speeds or depth, or covering varying amounts of ground, or presenting the subject in different ways in order to meet the needs of pupils who have reached different levels of achievement and help them make further progress. (2) Generally,

150

the use of a range of assessment instruments to determine how and in what ways pupils differ in their attainment from each other or a standard or norm.

ERA: Education Reform Act (1988).

Extended core: English, mathematics, science, technology and a modern language.

Foundation subjects: English, mathematics, science, technology (including design), history, geography, music, art and physical education, and also (for secondary-age pupils) a modern foreign language. Welsh is a foundation subject in schools in Wales which are not Welsh-speaking.

GCSE: *Mode 1*: Syllabuses are set and examinations conducted by the examining boards except for components such as course-work, and practical and oral work which are assessed by teachers subject to external moderation. *Mode 2*: Syllabuses are designed by schools with assessment conducted by the boards except for those elements which as for Mode 1 are suitable for internal assessment. *Mode 3*: Syllabuses are designed by schools and assessed by them subject to moderation by the boards. *Mixed mode*: This term is used to cover examinations which incorporate both Mode 1 and Mode 3 features.

Key stages: The periods in each pupil's education to which the elements of the national curriculum apply. There are four key stages, normally related to the age of the majority of the pupils in a teaching group. They are: KS1, 5-7; KS2, 7-11; KS3, 11-14; and KS4, 14-16. These are also known as reporting or assessment ages.

Levels of attainment: The 10 different levels of attainment, as proposed in the Task Group on Assessment and Testing (TGAT) report, covering the span of performances likely to be found from the first reporting age (7) to the last (16).

Modifications and disapplications: Terms used to describe various arrangements for lifting all or part of the national curriculum requirements for individuals, schools, or any other grouping specified by the Secretary of State for Education.

National curriculum (NC): The core and foundation subjects and their associated attainment targets, programmes of study, and assessment arrangements.

National Curriculum Council (NCC): Established under Section 14 of the Education Reform Act 1988 to keep all aspects of the curriculum for maintained schools under review and to advise the Secretary of State for Education on such matters; to advise on, and to carry out, programmes of research and development connected with the curriculum; and to publish and disseminate information relating to the curriculum for schools.

National Curriculum Development Plan: A coherent plan, made by each maintained school, identifying changes needed in curriculum, organisation, staffing arrangements, and in the allocation of non-teaching resources; setting out action needed to make those changes.

Profile components: Groups of attainment targets brought together for reporting purposes.

Programmes of study (POS): The matters, skills and processes which must be taught to pupils during each key stage in order for them to meet the objectives set out in the attainment targets.

School Examinations and Assessment Council (SEAC): Established under Sections 14 and 15 of the Education Reform Act 1988 to review and advise the Secretary of State for Education and the Secretary of State for Wales on matters relating to examinations and assessment arangements. Under Section 5 of the Education Reform Act, the SEAC is the body responsible for approving examination syllabuses for England and Wales.

Standard assessment tasks (SATs): Externally prescribed assessments which may incorporate a variety of assessment methods. They will complement the teachers' own assessments.

Statements of attainment (SOA): More precise objectives than the broader attainment targets, which will be defined within Statutory Orders. They are related to one of 10 levels of attainment on a single continuous scale, covering all four key stages.

Statutory Order: A statutory instrument which is regarded as an extension of the Education Reform Act 1988, enabling provisions of the Act to be augmented or updated.

Strands: A strand is a specific aspect or theme within a subject (for example, drama, or knowledge about language within English; communicating or handling information in information technology capability). Strands relate to progression, and particular strands can be identified running through the statements of attainment. In geography, strands do not appear in every attainment target and where they do appear are not regularly related to the number of statements at each level. For this reason, geography strands are identified by a letter following the statement.

Task Group on Assessment and Testing (TGAT): Established in October 1987 to advise the Secretary of State for Education on the practical considerations which should govern all assessment and testing within the national curriculum. TGAT submitted its main report in December 1987 and its supplementary reports in March 1988.

Whole curriculum: The curriculum of a school, incorporating the basic curriculum and all other provisions.

Source: National Curriculum Council/Department for Education, May 1992.

APPENDIX

TIMETABLE FOR THE INTRODUCTION OF THE NATIONAL CURRICULUM AND ASSESSMENT

		KS1	KS2	KS3	KS4
Mathematics	Introduction	1989	1990	1989	1992
and science	Assessment	1991	1994	1993	1994
English	Introduction	1989	1990	1990	1992
	Assessment	1991	1994	1993	1994
Technology	Introduction	1990	1990	1990	1993
	Assessment	1992	1994	1993	1995
History and	Introduction	1991	1991	1991	1994
geography	Assessment	1993	1995	1994	1996
Art, music,	Introduction	1992	1992	1992	1995
and PE	Assessment	1994	1996	1995	1997
Modern	Introduction	–	–	1992	1995
languages	Assessment	–	–	1995	1997

Source: NCC and SEAC 1992.
Note: Subjects are introduced in the autumn term; assessments are carried out in the summer term. Assessment dates for history, geography, art, music, PE, and modern languages are provisional.

INDEX